Folens

GCSE English for AQA/A

Keith Brindle • Roger Machin • Peter Thomas

United Kingdom: Folens Publishers, Apex Business Centre, Boscombe Road, Dunstable, LU5 4RL.
Email: folens@folens.com

Ireland: Folens Publishers, Greenhills Road, Tallaght, Dublin 24.
Email: info@folens.ie

Poland: JUKA, ul. Renesansowa 38, Warsaw 01-905.

Editor: Alison MacTier
Design and layout: 2idesign, Cambridge
Cover design: Duncan McTeer

First published 2002 by Folens Limited.
Reprinted 2003, 2004.

British Library Cataloguing in Publication Data. A catalogue record for this publication is available from the British Library.

ISBN 1 84303 245 7

Acknowledgements

Illustrations: pages 15, 30, 31 Jean de Lemos – Graham-Cameron Illustration; pages 86–87, 114–115, 120–121 Vanessa Lubach – Simon Girling Associates; pages 89, 104, 106–107 Brian Lee – Graham-Cameron Illustration; pages 116, 119, 158 Karen Perrins

Photographs: Cover images DigitalVision; pages 8–9 Corel; page 12 (top left) Bruce Ayres/Getty Images/Stone, (top right) Mirrorpix.com; page 13 DigitalVision; page 16 Popperfoto/PN2; page 19 Corbis; page 20 Peter Brooker/Rex Features; page 21 DigitalVision; pages 22–23 Robert Harding; page 26 Mirrorpix.com; pages 27, 28, 32 Corel; page 33 with thanks to Ruda Holiday Park; page 36 'Women! Cheaper Car Insurance' from *More*, 2–15 May 2001; page 37 'Thank Goodness for Kleenex' from *The Mirror Magazine*, 5 May 2001; page 38 PA Photos; pages 39, 40–41 DigitalVision; page 42 Frank Siteman/Getty Images/Stone; page 43 Rex Features; pages 44–45, 48, 50 DigitalVision; pages 52–53 Corel; pages 54–55 Moritz Steiger/Getty Images/The Image Bank; pages 56, 57 DigitalVision; page 58 *The Observer*; page 61 Don Bonsey/Getty Images/Stone; page 62 DigitalVision; pages 64–65 PA Photos; pages 67, 69, 70 DigitalVision; page 72 PA Photos; pages 73, 74–75, 76 DigitalVision; page 77 Corel; pages 78, 79 DigitalVision; page 80 Corel; pages 81, 82–83, 84, 85 DigitalVision; pages 86–87 Reuters; pages 90–93 (background) Digital Stock/Corbis, (figure) Caroline Wood/Getty Images/Stone; pages 94–95 Reuters; page 100 (top) PA Photos, (bottom) Popperfoto; pages 101–103, 108 Corel; pages 111, 112 Patrick Morin/Rex Features; pages 127–128 DigitalVision; pages 130–131 PhotoDisc/Getty Images; pages 136, 138, 140–141(Vivianne Moos) Rex Features; pages 142, 144 DigitalVision; page 146 © David Ellis. Reproduced courtesy of *CosmoGIRL!*; page 148 Jon Bradley/Getty Images/Stone; pages 152–3 DigitalVision; page 154 PhotoDisc/Getty Images; page 156 Corbis; pages 160, 162, 169, 170, 171 Corel

Text extracts: 'Saint Nick' from *Sky Customer Magazine*, December 2001, published by Redwood. 'Where the Law is not Blind to Colour' by Antonia Swinson from *The Daily Express*, 12 November 1987. 'Dating Skills' by Anita Singh from *Cosmopolitan*, January 2002. Courtesy of *Cosmopolitan* © National Magazine Company. Ruda Holiday brochure text – with thanks to Ruda Holiday Park. 'The rat-a-tat-tat of a doorstepper's revenge' from *The Sunday Times*, London, 20 January 2002. © Times Newspapers Limited, 2002. 'Caught in the middle' by Barbara Ellen from *The Observer*, 2 September 2001. © Barbara Ellen, 2001. Extract taken from the article 'Women with Rhyme, Reason and Rhythm' which appeared in *The Observer*, 4th November 2001, © Germaine Greer. 'Keep your hat on – it's only winter' by Elizabeth Heathcote from *The Independent on Sunday*, 16 December 2001. 'Island Man' by Grace Nichols from *I is a Long Memoried Woman* by Grace Nichols. Reproduced with permission of Curtis Brown Ltd, London, on behalf of Grace Nichols. © Grace Nichols, 1984. 'Blessing' by Imtiaz Dharker from *Postcards from God*, published by Bloodaxe Books. 'Two Scavengers In A Truck, Two Beautiful People In A Mercedes' by Lawrence Ferlinghetti, from *These Are My Rivers*, copyright © by Lawrence Ferlinghetti. Reprinted by permission of New Directions Publishing Corporation. 'What Were They Like?' by Denise Levertov from *Selected Poems*, published by Bloodaxe Books, reprinted by permission of Laurence Pollinger Ltd on behalf of the author and the proprietors, New Directions Publishing Corporation. 'Search For My Tongue' by Sujata Bhatt from *Brunizem* (1988) reprinted by permission of the publishers, Carcanet Press Limited. 'Unrelated Incidents' by Tom Leonard from *Intimate Voices: Selected Works 1965–1983*, published by Vintage. 'Half-Caste' by John Agard from *Get Back Pimple*, published by Penguin. 'Love After Love' by Derek Walcott from *Collected Poems 1948–1984*, reprinted by permission of the publishers, Faber and Faber Ltd. 'This Room' by Imtiaz Dharker from *I Speak for the Devil*, published by Bloodaxe Books. 'Not my Business' by Niyi Osundare from *Songs of the Seasons*, published by Heinemann Educational Books, Nigeria. *Kenneth William's Letters* edited by Russell Davies, published by HarperCollins Publishers. Reprinted by permission of HarperCollins Publishers Ltd. © The Estate of Kenneth Williams, 1994. 'Is this the Safest Hotel in the World?' by Robert Winder, from *Condé Nast Traveller*, January 2002. Robert Winder © Traveller/Condé Nast Publications Limited. 'Six words that rocked my world – "Your brother depends on you now"' by Susie Wood from *CosmoGIRL!*, November 2001. Courtesy of *CosmoGIRL!* © National Magazine Company. 'Fat, now it's his problem – "I starved myself down to 6¾ stone"' by Zoe Seymour from *She*, November 2001. Courtesy of *She* © National Magazine Company. *Diamond Dust* by Anita Desai, published by Vintage. Copyright © Anita Desai, 2000. Reproduced by permission of the author c/o Rogers, Coleridge & White Ltd., 20 Powis Mews, London W11 1JN. *Complicity* by Iain Banks, published by Little, Brown and Company. 'Iceberg in a bottle set to wash over UK' by Nikola Medic and Geoffrey Lean from *The Independent on Sunday*, 10 February 2002. 'Slowly but surely, Iceland is losing its ice' by Colin Woodard from *The San Francisco Chronicle*, 21 August 2000.

Welcome to Folens GCSE English for AQA/A!

The purpose of the book

This book will guide you through the skills and knowledge needed to gain the best possible grades in your GCSE English examination. It aims to show the key differences between one grade and the next, and to show you how to put this knowledge to your use.

How the book is structured

It is divided into four main sections dealing with Papers 1 and 2 of the exam. These are:

- Paper 1, Section A: Reading response to non-fiction and media texts
- Paper 1, Section B: Writing to argue, persuade and advise
- Paper 2, Section A: Reading response to poems from different cultures and traditions
- Paper 2, Section B: Writing to inform, explain and describe.

Slotted into these sections are additional units, dealing with key areas such as the planning process, or giving a brief tour of text types, to refresh your memory. The book ends with a full specimen paper, so you can experience the 'real thing' in advance of the actual date you complete the course.

Individual units

Depending on the sections of the exam, units deal with different skills and ideas, but some features occur consistently throughout most of the units:

- **'In this unit'** explains exactly what you will be covering.
- **'Where does it fit?'** explains which paper, which section and how much time is spent on the selected topic.
- **'Model'** or **'Source texts'**, often with useful annotations, show how professionals write.
- **'Developing skills and techniques'** takes you through the process in logical steps.
- **'Examiner's tip'** gives you inside information on how you can step up a grade.
- **'Extended practice'** gives you the opportunity to put all you have learned together.
- **'Key summary'** ends by summing up three or four main points of advice to remember.

The authors

The author team for this book is very well placed to guide you towards better grades in your exam. Keith Brindle is an experienced English teacher, writer and senior examiner. Peter Thomas works as a trainer of English teachers, and is also a senior examiner and writer. Roger Machin works as an English teacher, has written several GCSE study books, and has taught in a wide variety of schools in England and overseas. All in all, the perfect combination to help you fulfil your expectations.

Enjoy your study!

Contents

Your questions answered

What is a GCSE?

The letters stand for General Certificate of Secondary Education. GCSEs are available in almost every subject and most students finish them by the end of Year 11. The GCSEs you work towards and the number you take is usually decided at your school. Your GCSE results will be one of the most important factors in decisions you make about your future education and employment.

Which GCSEs are available in the subject area of English?

English and English Literature.

What's the difference between them?

The English GCSE is based on four skills areas: speaking, listening, reading and writing. You will be assessed on a wide range of tasks that reflect the different kinds of English we use.

The English Literature GCSE is based on prose, poetry and drama. You will be assessed on your ability to understand and interpret literary texts from each of these three areas.

Will I need to do any coursework?

Coursework accounts for 40% of your grade in English and 30% of your grade in English Literature.

What does the coursework consist of?

English		English Literature	
Speaking and listening	20%	Pre-1914 drama	10%
Shakespeare	5%	Pre-1914 prose	10%
Prose study	5%	Post-1914 drama	10%
Media	5%		
Original writing	5%		
Total	**40%**		**30%**

Will I need to take examinations?

Yes. The examination is worth 60% of your grade in English and 70% of your grade in English Literature.

English		**English Literature**	
Paper 1, Section A	15%	Paper 1, Section A	35%
Paper 1, Section B	15%	Paper 1, Section B	35%
Paper 2, Section A	15%		
Paper 2, Section B	15%		
Total	**60%**		**70%**

Is this a book about the GCSE English examination?

Yes. *GCSE English for AQA/A* will help you prepare for the examination in GCSE English. You will use other resources to help you with GCSE English coursework and with GCSE English Literature.

What will be in the GCSE English exam?

The English GCSE exam is an assessment of your reading and writing.

- Paper 1, Section A: reading of non-fiction and media texts
- Paper 1, Section B: writing to argue, persuade and advise
- Paper 2, Section A: reading of poems from different cultures and traditions
- Paper 2, Section B: writing to inform, explain and describe

How long is the GCSE English exam?

Paper 1 is 1 hour and 45 minutes long.
You will be advised to spend 1 hour on Section A and 45 minutes on Section B.

Paper 2 is 1 hour and 30 minutes long.
You will be advised to spend 45 minutes on Section A and 45 minutes on Section B.

How is *GCSE English for AQA/A* going to help me?

GCSE English for AQA/A is written by teachers and examiners who will help you achieve the highest grade you possibly can. It will provide you with all the skills, knowledge and practice you need to make you fully prepared for the GCSE English examination.

Paper 1, Section A: Reading response to non-fiction/media

Unit 1: **Types of texts**

In this unit you will:

- focus on the text types that might appear on Paper 1
- consider how they target purpose and audience
- examine their use of presentation and language
- complete practice tasks on a range of texts.

What will Paper 1, Section A, involve?

15% of your final marks are available for this section of the examination. It is a test of your reading ability.

You will spend about an hour analysing one, two or three non-fiction and/or media texts, which you have not seen previously.

Non-fiction and media texts

Non-fiction texts deal with real situations, events or people. They are likely to involve facts and opinions. They might report on something that has happened.

For example: autobiographical extracts; how the railways were born; the state of poverty in the Developing World.

They may attempt to argue, persuade or advise the reader.

For example: why should we be aware of the advantages and disadvantages of European integration? What makes a happy family? Why should safety rules be followed in science laboratories?

Media texts relate to some aspect of the communications media: newspapers, magazines, advertising, television, film, radio, the Internet and so on.

For example: articles and reports; reviews of programmes or movies; web pages; advertising fliers.

Often, of course, texts on the examination paper will be non-fiction *and* involve the media.

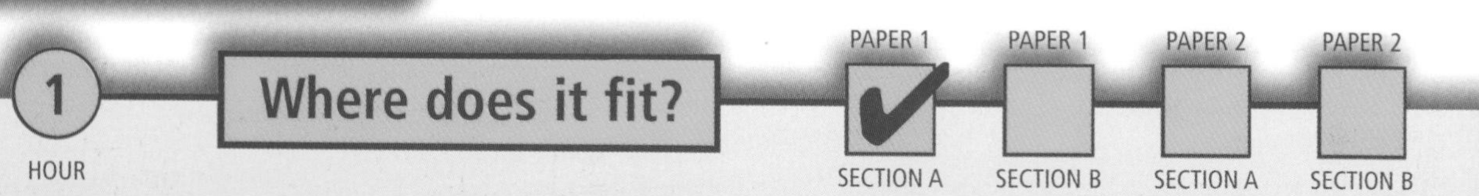

To examine the texts, you will be concentrating on:

- their purposes – *what forms of text they are and what they are trying to do*
- their audiences – *who they are written for*
- what they have to say – *the message or messages in the texts*
- how they get their message across – *the use of ideas, details, language and presentational devices.*

These elements will be closely related.

You will be expected to recognise *what* a writer is trying to do, *why* and *how*. There will also be a need to compare texts, cross-referencing details and ideas. Knowledge of different text types, therefore, is essential if you wish to be successful.

EXAMINER'S TIP

Teachers can explain how to examine texts and can give you the vocabulary needed to write about them. However, answers produced in the examination usually reveal which students have also read widely. They analyse more and cope better with textual complexities.

For example, in the mark scheme it states:

Grade C: clear *attempt* to deal with the material.
Grade A: a *full understanding* of what is being asked.

Wider reading is likely to give you easier access to the higher grades.

TASK 1

a. Write a list of the different types of text you have read in your free time in the past two weeks.

Write approximately how long you have spent reading each text type.

Give the purpose and audience of each text. For example:

Text	Time	Purpose	Audience
Back page of newspaper	30 minutes	Find out soccer results	Football fan, like me

b. Have you been reading widely and regularly?

TASK 2

a. Examine these extracts. For each one, decide:
- whether it is a non-fiction or media text
- what its purpose and audience is.

How have presentational and linguistic devices influenced your decision? Look at the visual impressions created and how language is used.

1.

Vaccination programme set to fail

reports Health Correspondent Kieron Black

Health chiefs came under attack from opposition politicians yesterday, as figures emerged which seemed to indicate that cases of flu are increasing. "Not enough people at risk have been vaccinated," said… .

2.

It's a Breeze!

It's elegant …
Rich and smooth …
Free from any stress …
Alone and alive …

3.

Back Forward Stop Refresh Home AutoFill

Address: go

Lyoos : Your Personal Internet Guide 2idesign mnemonic9

Favorites History Search Scrapbook

Games, games, games. All you need at the lowest prices. Check out www.cheepies.com

This is the Games Zone.

Zap 'em!

4.

When he was at school, no one could have guessed he would later find his career in the theatre. If it had been suggested, they might have pointed out his poor health, and said that he needed an operation or two, to allow him to lead a more normal life; but the fact that he now performs on West End stages and before a movie audience of millions will have surprised more than a few.

In each of the examples you have looked at, layout and language have been chosen carefully to produce a desired effect.

In the following example, a student has attempted to write for a set purpose and audience, but has not been thoroughly convincing!

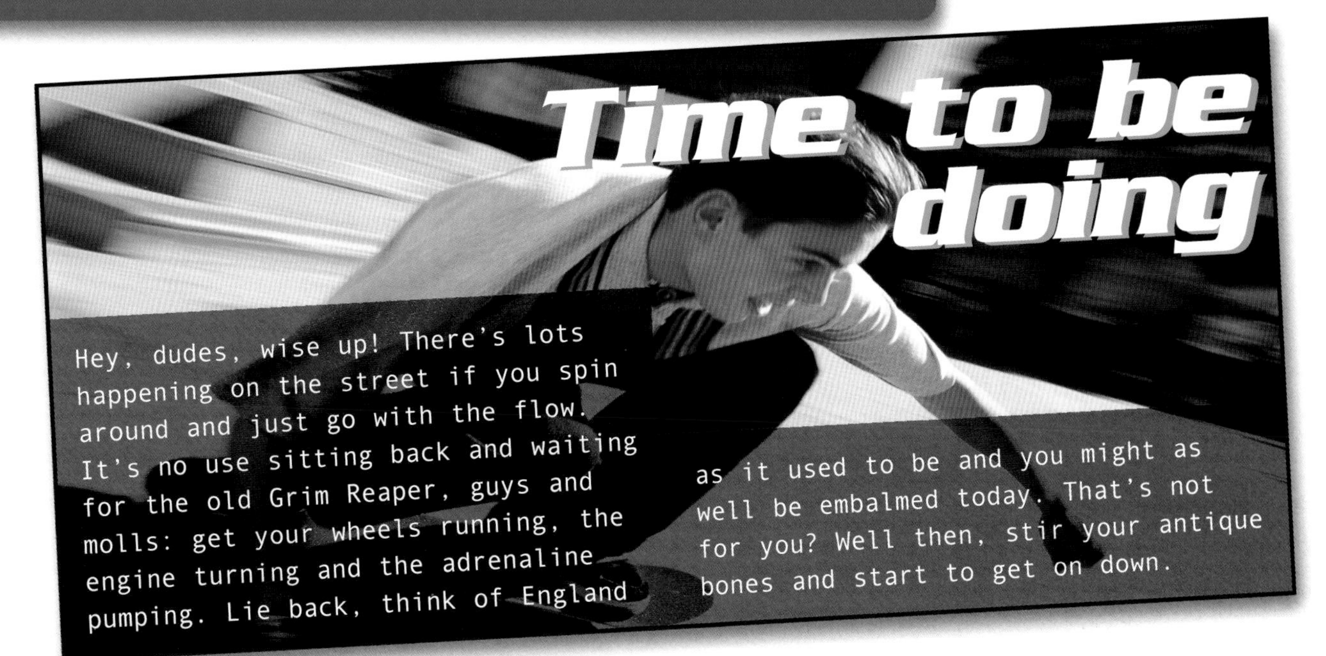

TASK 3

The task the student had was to write an introduction to a newspaper article for Senior Citizens about local activities they might enjoy.

To make it appropriate for purpose and audience:

a. re-design the layout (a sketch willl do)
b. re-write the text.

You might wish to change the:

- headline
- text layout
- language.

You might wish to add a:

- by-line
- strap line
- caption.

You might begin:

It really is possible to enjoy your life as a Senior Citizen … .

KEY SUMMARY

To be properly prepared for Paper 1, Section A, you need a good working knowledge of:

- different text types
- how they are designed for purpose and audience.

Unit 2: **Inferences, facts and opinions**

In this unit you will:

- focus on two Assessment Objectives for Reading and how to:
  - interpret texts
  - refer appropriately to them
  - deal with facts and opinions
- practise necessary skills
- analyse a variety of texts, including: an article from a women's magazine published in 1935, an advertising feature from *Sky Customer Magazine* and a review from the *Daily Express*.

What are Assessment Objectives?

Assessment Objectives are the skills that the examination is testing. In this case, we are dealing with Reading Objectives.

With which Assessment Objectives are we dealing?

Candidates are required to demonstrate their ability to:

1. **read, with insight and engagement, making appropriate references to texts and developing and sustaining interpretations of them**

   For the examination, you need to be able to:
   → understand and explain the full meaning of texts
   → refer to texts, using appropriate detail and quoting when necessary

2. **distinguish between fact and opinion and evaluate how information is presented.**

   For the examination, you need to be able to:
   → identify facts and opinions
   → explain how they are used by writers to further their purposes.

These skills will be tested in Paper 1, Section A, where you will be presented with two or three texts and will answer a number of questions about them.

You will have about an hour to complete the work.

1 HOUR

Where does it fit?

PAPER 1	PAPER 1	PAPER 2	PAPER 2
✔			
SECTION A	SECTION B	SECTION A	SECTION B

Working with objectives

Assessment Objective 1

Candidates are required to demonstrate their ability to read, with insight and engagement, making appropriate references to texts and developing and sustaining interpretations of them.

Reading with insight and engagement

You will be expected to understand and explain inferences in texts. Rather than repeating textual detail, you must explain what is **implied** or **suggested**. For example, we do not always say what we mean:

The fireman seems to praise the boy, when he says, "Who's a clever boy then?" However, he is being ironic.

You must be able to select relevant material to prove your point, quoting when necessary. Sometimes you might mention examples:

Clearly she watches soap operas, because she knows all about *Coronation Street*.

At other times, you will quote:

The advertisers use humour to persuade us that Goldilox is quality hair colourant: 'Your hair'll be so perfect, they'll *bearly* believe it!'

Developing and sustaining interpretations

You will have to write about the purpose of texts, expanding upon and linking ideas – perhaps explaining, in your own words, how impressions are created or themes developed:

Grade F:

The writer of the letter says there are problems when travelling by train. He says how he went across the desert by camel. He thinks things can get better ... .

Grade A:

The writer produces a convincing argument, claiming that rail travel abroad is dangerous and needs to improve. He compares the route through central Europe with a camel trek across the desert, making the point that camels can be safer and implying, no doubt with tongue in cheek, that they produce more comfortable rides than many carriage seats: 'which bruised my bottom horribly'.

TASK 1

Why, exactly, is the second answer better?

Source text

Now read this longer text, which is similar to the sort you will encounter in the exam.

It is an extract from *Woman's Magazine Annual 1935*. As you will see, girls did not always have the same opportunities as boys.

Banking – As a Career for Girls

In this article I want to show that, contrary to popular opinion, banking offers definite scope for the girl with ambition and ability.

Five years ago I could not have made this statement with any sincerity. At that time the dizziest height that any girl bank clerk could hope to attain was that of being a secretary to a director, a manager or a superintendent. It is almost superfluous to add that the number of these positions was strictly limited.

Today, resultant on the complete mechanisation of banking, there are bright prospects for women in the world of cheques. By proving conclusively that they are vastly superior to men in the business of working machines, the feminine staffs of the big banks are rapidly gaining recognition from the managements … .

Combining as it does security of tenure, pensions at fifty years of age, good working conditions and hours and a reasonable salary (even the rank and file are paid on average £4 a week), banking is, I submit, an ideal career for a girl.

To the usual charge that the work is dull I can state only that using an adding machine is no more boring than using a typewriter and is not nearly so difficult.

TASK 2

a. How does the writer create the impression that banking is a good choice for girls?

To show you understand the inferences, comment on words, phrases or sentences that are positive.

- Write about: words like 'ideal', phrases like 'bright prospects for women', and sentences like the one that begins, 'Combining as it does security of tenure… '.

Quote appropriately, to illustrate your points.

Consider the whole article, paying particular attention to the opening and ending.

b. What does the text suggest about the role of women in the 1930s?

Assessment Objective 2

Candidates are required to demonstrate their ability to distinguish between fact and opinion and evaluate how information is presented.

Fact and opinion

Facts can be proven. Often, they will involve figures. They are true, beyond any reasonable doubt.

Opinions are what people think or believe. They are interpretations. They could be correct, but can be challenged by someone with a different opinion.

Sometimes it can be difficult to tell the difference between a fact and an opinion:
It is the most successful basketball team in the world.

This is probably an opinion, which depends upon someone's interpretation of 'successful'. However, it could follow a list of facts that would seem to prove the point! For example, a list of baskets scored or income received.

In the examination, however, it is likely that you will be asked to locate facts and opinions and say how they are used. Consequently, you will be able to choose details about which you are confident, and will have the opportunity to explain your choices.

How are facts and opinions used?
Consider how **facts** are used in the following example:
Output has risen by 37%; labour costs have fallen by 8%; profits have risen by 23% during the year. The prospects for the company seem… .

The final sentence is unfinished, but it is likely that prospects seem good. How do we know? The facts suggest that the company is becoming more efficient ('output has risen/costs have fallen'), and if profits are rising, there is nothing here to suggest any reversal in the future.

Facts have been used to present a positive picture of the company, and nothing has been included to counter that impression.

EXAMINER'S TIP

Many candidates find it difficult to explain how facts and opinions are used. When writing about them, try to do more than just identify them. For good marks, explain:

- what they are *suggesting*
- what *effect* they are intended to have on the reader.

For example, if we read:

48% of people enjoy Weetabix!, do we think: 'Then 52% don't?'

or, does:

It's the best-selling car in its class! make us wonder: 'How many others are in its class?'

TASK 3

How are facts used here?

Not surprisingly, recent surveys have confirmed that it is more expensive to eat out at motorway service areas than in city centre snack bars. Customers confirmed that they expect to pay up to 30% more.

Opinions are also employed to illustrate points or support a writer's theory.

Consider this statement:
The new development is big, brash and beautiful.

This is clearly an opinion, since there is no definite proof: 'big', for example means different things – a 'big problem' is very different from a 'big lake'; 'brash' implies criticism, but is only what someone thinks; and beauty is always 'in the eye of the beholder'.

The writer is presenting the development as eye-catching, and the **alliteration** makes it appear dynamic, as if energy is bursting out of it. It seems modern ('brash'), yet still something to admire ('beautiful').

TASK 4

How is opinion used in the following statements?

a. *Books are a waste of time and space. Almost everyone prefers movies to reading stories, and computers provide information that's more detailed and reliable than details you find in a conventional library.*

b. *Surely, everyone agrees that Michael Owen is like a silky predator in the penalty area.*

Usually, **facts** and **opinions** are blended in texts:

fact

opinion

I have been dating men for over 37 years, and I can honestly say that very few understand the psychological importance of shopping.

Here, a **fact** – '37 years' – has been used to give the writer and her opinions credibility. If she has so much experience, she ought to know what she is talking about!

Her **opinion**, then, might be taken more seriously when she claims that men do not realise why shopping is so important. She is more likely to be believed.

TASK 5

Read this extract.

The world has definitely changed for the worse. My grandmother, who was Victorian and therefore held strict moral values, could detail the deterioration that had occurred during her 92 years. Sometimes, she annoyed people, but that is not to say she was incorrect in what she said. She knew, for example, that raising children need not be as difficult as people claim, and that the way many people behave nowadays is not only unacceptable but also unnecessary. As I think about her family – my seven fine uncles and aunts – she does seem to have had a point.

a. List the facts and the opinions.

b. Explain how they have been used, identifying the:
- writer's purpose
- effect that is created.

c. Write a brief response in which you refute the writer's claims.
- Blend facts and opinions in your writing.

d. Explain how you have used facts and opinions.

Evaluating how information is presented

To **evaluate** means to 'judge' or 'assess'.

When deciding whether a writer has been successful in the use of facts and opinions, we have to consider how convincing the text seems in terms of:

- how appropriate it is for its audience
- how well it has fulfilled its purpose.

In other words, have the facts and opinions been effective in fulfilling the writer's aims?

EXAMINER'S TIP

A personal response from candidates is welcomed: it shows they are 'engaging' with the text. However, any comments *must* be based on the text, because we are dealing with reading ability. Always ensure you are analysing what has been written, and not putting forward a different theory of your own.

TASK 6

a. What is the purpose and audience for this advertising feature from *Sky Customer Magazine*?

b. How successfully are facts and opinions used?

Saint Nick

Nickelodeon (Channel 604) has got some great **Thank Nick It's Fridays** lined up this month. Best of the bunch has to be the 'Music 'n' Magic' special from 3.30pm on Friday 7th. The music will be provided by hip-hop's newest kid on the block L'il Bow Wow and teen popster Aaron Carter – their concert specials will be popping up in-between episodes of the magical *Sabrina The Teenage Witch*. And, as ever with Nickelodeon, there'll also be the chance to win some fantastic prizes, such as a sleepover at Hamleys toy store for you and your friends.

A candidate's response

One student wrote:

The feature is clearly aimed at young people. They are the ones who watch Nickelodeon; and adults are hardly likely to want to sleep over at Hamleys toy store! The writer wants children to watch 'Thank God It's Nick' and tries to interest them in what it has to offer.

The facts tell readers what the programme has to offer; not just when it is transmitted, but that it features performers like L'il Bow Wow, Aaron Carter and Sabrina. In a final attempt to capture the imagination, it ends by stressing the prizes that can be won by viewers. The writer is attempting to make the programme sound full of music, stars and opportunity.

However, opinions are also used throughout, to influence how readers perceive the facts. The programmes are 'great', and the prizes are 'fantastic'. Using such informal language is likely to appeal to the intended audience and influence its opinion. In a further attempt to capture the audience – presumably so that children will watch throughout December – the writer gives an opinion that the first edition is the best:

> 'Best of the bunch has to be the 'Music 'n' Magic' special from 3.30pm on Friday 7th.'

The feature is appropriate and likely to be successful. Its brevity, the relatively limited but attractive facts and the simple way the programme is assessed ('great') will appeal to young people.

TASK 7

Working with a friend, decide whether this answer:

- distinguishes between fact and opinion
- evaluates how the information is presented
- shows insight and engagement
- makes appropriate references to the text
- develops and sustains an interpretation.

Extended practice

TASK 8

Read the following review and answer the questions, including appropriate references to the text.

Where the Law is not Blind to Colour

by Antonia Swinson

'We are supposed to be vicious and cruel,' said a black inmate on Death Row, 'but this goes beyond anything we'd ever do.'

Last night's documentary *Fourteen Days in May* (BBC1, 9.30pm) recorded the final 14 days earlier this year in the life of Edward Earl Johnson, a Mississippi black man convicted on a charge of murdering a white policeman and attempted assault on a white woman.

Mistake

At 26, Edward had already been waiting to die for eight years. He was articulate, from a good family – his mother is a Law Enforcement Officer – and had no previous record.

His mistake had been to sign a false confession dictated at the roadside by two white police officers.

Justice, we learned, is not colour blind.

The programme cited a recent survey which found that a black man convicted for killing a white man is four times more likely to receive the death sentence than a white man.

Then there is the problem of money.

As a Superintendent of the Penitentiary admitted, there is a different quality of justice obtained from a good private lawyer, than from a public attorney paid by the State.

If you are poor as well as black, you haven't a chance.

Where I admired – I couldn't say enjoyed – the programme so much was that the interviewer was as unobtrusive as a fly on the wall.

There was neither schmaltz nor stupid

questions. The characters in this tragedy – for that is what it was – were allowed to speak for themselves.

We saw the testing of the equipment, when two black rabbits, noses still twitching, were gassed. Then there was the sad irony of Edward's mother embracing the prison staff.

Underneath it all, there was the firm belief in Edward's innocence. When his laid-back lawyer received the final news that there would be no stay of execution, he simply shrugged: 'That's the end of that.'

But to me it seemed as if that was just the beginning. Johnson died.

Next day, the Superintendent, who had earlier had 'no problem' with the prisoner's guilt, had to face the Press, and say that he had protested his innocence to the end.

The Superintendent looked shaken, and full of doubt.

Murder

Since then, a woman has come forward who says she was with Johnson on the night of the murder. She claimed she had earlier told a white Law Enforcement Officer, but had been told to mind her own business.

So how certain of a person's guilt do we have to be before they are executed?

I don't know the answer, but this magnificent programme at least had the guts to ask the question.

Daily Express

QUESTIONS

Remember to make appropriate reference to the article.

a. What is the text's purpose and audience?

As part of your response to purpose, discuss Swinson's attitude to the programme.

b. How are facts and opinions used?

c. How successful is the writer in achieving her aims?

KEY SUMMARY

To be successful in the examination, you need the ability to:

- engage with texts, understanding implications
- analyse whole texts and their purposes
- make appropriate references
- explain how facts and opinions are used
- judge how successful writers have been in achieving their purposes.

Unit 3: **Following arguments and language use**

In this unit you will:

- focus on two Assessment Objectives for Reading, related to following an argument and examining the effects of language
- consider how best to respond to their demands
- revise an analytical vocabulary
- complete a number of tasks, practising the skills required
- analyse a variety of texts, including: a letter, an article from *Cosmopolitan*, advertisements, autobiographies and a holiday brochure.

Which Assessment Objectives are we dealing with here?

Candidates are required to demonstrate their ability to:

1. follow an argument, identifying implications and recognising inconsistencies

For the examination, you need to be able to:

→ understand the main points in an argument
→ analyse what the writer is suggesting
→ select and discuss any change in opinion or any point that seems contradictory
→ explain how an argument has been constructed.

2. understand and evaluate how writers use linguistic, structural and presentational devices to achieve their effects, and comment on the ways in which language varies and changes.

For the examination, you need to be able to:

→ understand how writers use language to structure their writing
→ comment on structural devices and the effectiveness of presentational devices, like pictures, headlines and so on (*see Unit 4*)
→ analyse the linguistic content of texts.

These skills will be tested in Paper 1, Section A, where you will be presented with two or three texts and will answer a number of questions on them.

You will have about an hour to complete the work.

1 HOUR — **Where does it fit?** — PAPER 1 SECTION A ✔ | PAPER 1 SECTION B | PAPER 2 SECTION A | PAPER 2 SECTION B

Working with objectives

Assessment Objective 1
Candidates are required to demonstrate their ability to follow an argument, identifying implications and recognising inconsistencies

Following an argument

Following an argument does not just mean understanding what is said and in what order. Such **paraphrase** usually results in a grade in the G to D range. To achieve higher grades, candidates need to show *how* the argument has been constructed to gain its effect. To do this, an appropriate vocabulary is needed.

Arguments will, typically, use:
- an **introduction** to the topic
- a logical **development**, so that the reader moves from one point to another without confusion
- **discourse markers** to link points: *therefore, however, consequently, on the other hand, surprisingly, what is more, furthermore, in addition,* and so on
- **facts** and **opinions**
- a **conclusion** that sums up the writer's opinions.

Often, there will be other techniques, including:
- contrasts
- examples
- anecdotes
- quotation
- irony
- rhetoric
- balance
- contradictions
- summaries.

We also need to be aware of:
- the writer's tone – whether, for instance, the argument is **subtle**:

  a. *Viewers might think it worthwhile to consider exactly what their children might be watching before selecting their evening's viewing.*

  b. *There is too much sex on television. Broadcasters ignore their moral responsibilities.*

  In a, the writer uses 'might' to coax readers into agreeing with his views.

  In b, the writer sounds definite and allows no room for disagreement.

- the precise language used – whether it is formal, informal, poetic, emotive, challenging, conversational, complex, abstract, hypothetical, literary, violent, ironic and so on.

EXAMINER'S TIP

With any of these terms, it is not enough simply to **identify** them.

The best candidates explain *why* an effect is used, and *what* its effect is.

Source text

This is the opening of a letter arguing that the improvement of the railways is vital for Britain in the Twenty-first Century:

Dear Prime Minister,

According to my next-door neighbour, there is nothing wrong with our railways. Of course, she is housebound and has not travelled further than the living room for ten years. If she, like me, had to suffer price increases, delays, overcrowding, and dirty carriages each day, she would, no doubt, be singing from a different hymn sheet.

The government says it must be 'prudent with the public purse'. Yet it found hundreds of millions for the Millennium Dome; can afford to spend a fortune on weapons systems, computers that do not work, committees that talk expensively and to no effect, and on jaunts to conferences around the globe; but still cannot find enough cash to revitalise our ailing rail network.

Are you utterly short-sighted? Do you ever consider the real needs of the people of this country?

- irony
- introduction to line of argument
- quotation/ one viewpoint
- metaphor
- discourse marker
- contrasting list for effect
- emotive language
- rhetoric

Asked to follow how the argument had been presented, an A Grade candidate began:

The writer introduces her topic by using the ironic example of her next-door neighbour who, it seems, is happy with the railways; but the reader smiles when it is pointed out that her neighbour is not able to use them. We learn that if the writer's neighbour tried to travel by rail, she would encounter the problems that are the writer's major concern and have been listed at the start of the letter to make them sound considerable:

'price increases, delays, overcrowding… '.

TASK 1

Continue this analysis of the letter extract.

Identifying implications and recognising inconsistencies

Implication means 'what the writer is suggesting'; to **identify implications** means to read beyond the surface level of the text.

Explaining deeper meaning helps you move to higher grades.

For example: *She is like a butterfly, flitting from one task to another.*

We are given the impression that she is beautiful and delicate ('butterfly'), and that she moves easily from one job to the next.

Or, with a different interpretation:

She seems light ('butterfly'), as if her actions are temporary and meaningless. We learn she 'flits' between jobs, suggesting she does not apply herself, does not stay very long in one place, and, presumably, has little effect upon anything she touches.

Inconsistency is when a point of view changes or when there is a contradiction – when comparing different texts (*See Unit 4*), it could be when two writers simply disagree. Sometimes, however, it can be a technique used by writers to surprise, or to balance an argument:

Some point out that children are perfectly safe on the streets, and that violent attacks in those circumstances have not increased during the past thirty years. However, that is a ridiculous argument.

or it might be a time when the argument seems to contradict itself:

Thankfully, in this area there have been no child murders in the last decade. Yet, police figures released last week show a 63% increase in attacks on young people.

TASK 2

Explain the effects produced by the writer in the last two examples.

Source text

This extract is from an article in which the writer argues that women can improve their chances of attracting the man of their choice, and offers advice on how to be successful.

The eyes have it*

Eyes are the cornerstone of body language and the key to attracting him. "If you're listening well, your body language is a mirror of what the other person is saying," says Quilliam. Make eye contact to make the subliminal point that you 'click' and are worth getting to know. "Don't worry if he looks away – he may have to in order to think – but keep your gaze on his face," she explains. Glancing down occasionally and fluttering your eyelashes are classic flirt signals guaranteed to get his pulse racing. Also, when you're attracted to someone, your pupils dilate and men subconsciously pick up on that signal, too. "While you can't consciously control your pupils, they do dilate in a dark environment," explains Dr Bull. "So opt for clubs and bars that are dimly lit. Your pupils will look huge, and by appearing attracted to the man you're after, he'll be attracted to you."

Cosmopolitan, January 2002

sentence introduces topic

pun used to attract attention (*phrase used in parliament following a vote by MPs)

development: another expert quoted

expert quoted

positive conclusion that links with opening

apparent inconsistencies but adding to general advice

TASK 3

a. How does this text develop?

In your answer, discuss:

- how the purpose is apparent in the opening and ending
- the points made and how they are linked
- any inconsistencies.

b. What is implied about the kind of audience for this article?

Consider:

- recommended courses of action (for example 'flirt', 'fluttering')
- suggested rendezvous (for example 'clubs and bars')
- the language used (for example 'The eyes have it', 'subliminal', 'dilate' and the imperative tone in places: 'Don't worry', 'opt').

Assessment Objective 2
Candidates are required to demonstrate their ability to understand and evaluate how writers use linguistic … devices to achieve their effects, and comment on ways language varies and changes.

Using linguistic devices

Writers use a wide range of techniques to achieve their purposes and convince audiences.

In the examination, candidates need to recognise linguistic devices and say how they are used.

They must be able to:
- identify discourse markers, imperatives, formal and informal terms, irony, rhetoric and so on
- explain the effect they produce.

EXAMINER'S TIP

When dealing with poetry and prose texts for English Paper 2 or in GCSE English Literature, candidates may discuss similes, metaphors, alliteration and so on, and explain how they are used. It is noticeable, however, that relatively few transfer those skills to Section A of Paper 1, when they are dealing with 'unseen' texts.

Those who can examine language in the same way on Paper 1 are rewarded.

Since language can be used in many different ways, it is not possible to have a complete 'checklist' of devices.

Some techniques, however, will occur regularly.

For example:

Figurative language

'Eyes are the cornerstone of body language and the key to attracting him.'

The writer uses two metaphors to give eyes the impression of importance – firstly, 'cornerstone' – and, to show that they can 'unlock' a world of treasure, 'key'… .

Formal and informal language

'Make eye contact to make a subliminal point that you "click"… .'

In this instance, the writer uses formal and complex language ('subliminal point') to suggest that she is an expert, but then includes the term 'click', which is placed in inverted commas, to show it is a conversational term. It indicates that the writer is 'in touch' with the way women talk to each other.

Revising useful language terms

You have probably looked at these terms many times during English lessons, but it is useful to revise what you know when preparing for this section of the exam.

TASK 4

Match the linguistic devices with the examples 'a' to 'j' and write a brief explanation of the effect achieved in each case. In some instances, more than one device will have been used in the same quotation.

Linguistic devices

- humour
- irony – *subtle mockery*
- bathos – *descending from the grand to the everyday*
- exaggeration
- listing
- repetition
- complex sentence
- simple sentence
- rhetoric – *language used for effect, not requiring a direct response*
- emotive language – *touching the emotions*
- an imperative – *demanding action*
- colloquial – *conversational*
- ambiguity – *where more than one interpretation is possible*
- contrast
- discourse marker – *word or phrase joining ideas logically*

a. 'I called the agency. I paid the money. I waited patiently. Did the tickets arrive? They did not! I even turned the postman upside down and shook him, but it did no good.'

b. 'Throughout the night, the two girls sat beside the old woman, bathing her wounds and talking to her, endeavouring to keep her spirit alive. Sadly, they failed.'

c. 'If a company is in trouble, sack some workers; if a director fails, give him half a million pounds and find him another job.'

d. 'It's chewy, it's cheery, it's the choice of chappies from Cheshire. It's tremendous!'

e. 'The Head of Research was able to prove conclusively that the bacteria will, ultimately, reach the food chain. As a result, millions will die. Tragic, eh? Sad, or what? Well, yes, actually, it is if you happen to live in that region of Africa. Very sad.'

f. 'She seemed to have the world at her feet, floating above her contemporaries with imperious ease – until, that is, the bubble burst and she landed in the metaphorical equivalent of a dung heap.'

g. 'Sir Robert is a magistrate and not the sort of man to take things lying down. So, I was devastated to find him on his back in the cabbage patch.'

h. 'Kerry Watts deserves every honour the sport can bestow on her. After all, she did manage to finish above the competitor from the Faroe Islands.'

i. 'Can you imagine a more prophetic gesture? When he raised his two fingers, he was not to know that, within days, two judgments would fall upon him: he was suspended from all duties at the nursing home; and then lost custody of his stepchildren.'

j. 'Every hour I utter a silent prayer, to say "thank you" for what has happened. Those poor souls would still have been grubbing in the dirt of the shanty town if your organisation had not come along when it did; had not given them hope and, indeed, a sense of purpose; had not provided them with clothes, a home and a future, which meant they could leave the "protection" of the kindly agency that had made their lives a misery for more than eighteen months. You have saved them.'

Commenting on how language varies and changes

Language is used differently, depending on the situation. Consider, for instance, these greetings:

a. *'How wonderful to see you, darling.'*
b. *'Hello. Let's get started. Settle yourselves. Quickly.'*
c. *'Watcha.'*
d. *'Good morrow, my Lord.'*
e. *'Good morning, Year 10. And may I say what a pleasure it is to meet you.'*
f. *'Nyergh!'*

TASK 5

Discuss with a partner what sorts of people are speaking, or in what situations, and explain your answers.

In each case, we can visualise the speaker.

Writers use shifts in language to generate particular effects.

This is from a **car advertisement**:

This will be the most comfortable car ride you have ever enjoyed. The re-designed suspension system, created in Chicago by Spelador, literally demands a suspension of belief.

'Oh, yes. As if I'd believe that.'

Certainly, you may scoff: but a test drive will erase all doubts.

When the readers recognise the voice of a cynical customer, it probably represents their own feeling. This involves the readers, who are engaged in a kind of conversation; the advertiser has the readers' attention, and can then move on to further persuasion.

In this **autobiography**, the author reflects on his upbringing in Yorkshire, using colloquial terms to help create a picture of his life in the 1950s. The language used then contrasts with the way in which the author writes now, suggesting how much he has changed:

> *If I failed to eat my lunch, there was trouble. Mum glowered.*
>
> *"What's up wi' thee? Tha's bin aytin' spogs again, I'll bet!"*
>
> *'Spogs' – sweets – were always a cause of consternation at that stage in my life. I loved eating them, and if 'aytin' 'em' meant I got bad teeth, it seemed worth the pain.*
>
> From *Days on Lupset* by W Chantry

Extended practice

Consider the following extracts. They are taken from different sections of a brochure advertising a holiday park in Devon.

Ruda Holiday Park is practically on the beach – and what a beach. Set in the centre of seven miles of the most glorious sand that the West Country has to offer is the jewel in the crown of the Golden Coast – Croyde Bay.

Judged time and again by the English Tourist Board as the Best Holiday Park in the West Country – and by the families who return to Ruda year after year. Few Holiday Parks can boast such a magnificent setting.

At Ruda Holiday Park there's always something to do. The kids may be off with a whole gang on a supervised rockpool expedition while you laze around with an ice-cream at the beach bar or you may be swirling round the rapids ride in Cascades while the kids rehearse for a talent night. Whatever you fancy, whatever your age, there's always so much to do at Ruda.

TASK 6

a. What similarities do you find in the language used in the two extracts?

b. Explain any differences.

You might wish to discuss, for example, the use and effect of:

- adjectives
- figurative language
- third and second person narrative.
- colloquialisms
- repetition

KEY SUMMARY

You must be able to explain:

- how an argument is constructed, using appropriate terminology
- what writers are suggesting and the effects of inconsistencies
- how linguistic devices are used
- how language varies and changes.

Comment should be detailed and precise.

Unit 4: Comparison of texts and presentational devices

In this unit you will:

- focus on two Assessment Objectives for Reading, dealing with structural and presentational devices and how to compare texts
- concentrate on non-fiction and media texts
- practise using appropriate vocabulary for tasks involving presentation and comparison
- focus on a variety of texts, including: advertisements, a newspaper report, a flier, an article from *The Sunday Times* and a letter.

With which Assessment Objectives are we dealing?

Candidates are required to demonstrate their ability to:

1. **understand how writers use … structural and presentational devices to achieve their effects…**

> For the examination, you need to be able to:
> → explain how a text has been constructed, and for what purpose
> → analyse the effectiveness of presentational devices like pictures, headlines, and so on.

2. **select material appropriate to their purpose, collate material from different sources, and make cross-references.**

> For the examination, you need to be able to:
> → refer to the text to illustrate points you make
> → deal with material from different texts
> → compare texts, making direct comparisons of significant features.

Candidates are tested on both non-fiction and media texts. Appropriate technical vocabulary is needed, especially in order to deal with media concepts.

These skills will be tested in Paper 1, Section A, where you will be presented with two or three texts and will answer a number of questions on them.

You will have about an hour to complete the work.

1 HOUR — **Where does it fit?**

PAPER 1	PAPER 1	PAPER 2	PAPER 2
✔			
SECTION A	SECTION B	SECTION A	SECTION B

Working with objectives

Assessment Objective 1
Candidates are required to demonstrate their ability to understand how writers use ... structural and presentational devices to achieve their effects... .

Structural devices

Structural devices are the 'building blocks' of the text – elements such as:

- paragraphs
- sub-headings
- bulleted lists
- text boxes
- the order information is presented.

Presentational devices

Presentational devices are the obviously visual elements of texts, such as:
text boxes, sub-headings and bullets, as well as photographs (long, medium, close-up, in sharp focus and soft focus shots), designs, illustrations, graphs, diagrams, cartoons, headlines, sub-headings, strap lines, by-lines, captions, columns, fonts (bold, italic, and so on), brand names, logos, slogans, and the use of colour and layout.

TASK 1

Discuss with a partner what each of the above terms means. Use a dictionary or other source if you are unsure.

EXAMINER'S TIP

Candidates are often able to list presentational features in texts. However, to reach higher grades, you must write about the **effect** of the devices:

- why they are used
- how they are used
- how effective they are.

For example, the mark scheme states:

Grade A: <u>analyses</u> a range of presentational devices and layout.

Source text

This is an advertisement from a women's magazine:

TASK 2

In answering the following questions, concentrate on structural and presentational devices, rather than on the language used.

a. What is the effect of the picture? How might it appeal to the target audience? Say exactly what it reveals, what is not included, and why it has been presented in this way.

b. Why have these particular colours been chosen for the advertisement? Try to say what the colours suggest and their likely appeal.

c. How has the name of the company been identified clearly? Discuss its positioning, the design, font style and so on.

d. What is the audience likely to remember most about the advertisement? Explain why. You may wish to mention some features not previously analysed, such as the balance between picture and advertising copy (text), and what stands out most prominently.

e. Will the advertisement be successful? Why/why not? Give a personal opinion, but base it firmly upon features of the advertisement.

A candidate's response

An A Grade candidate was asked to consider:
- the target audience for this advertisement
- its presentational devices
- its success.

The advertisement is clearly aimed at young people. The largest font emphasises the text message, which is a mode of communication associated with young people; in fact, the mobile phone itself is the main image. It is surrounded by blue denim, which might also be associated with teenagers. The colour mirrors the blue on the packet of Kleenex tissues, linking the sad experience (the lover has found someone else) with a product which, it is implied, is essential at such times.

TASK 3

a. List any further presentational devices.

b. Complete this answer, analysing all the relevant devices.

Assessment Objective 2
Candidates are required to demonstrate their ability to select material appropriate to their purpose, collate material from different sources, and make cross-references.

In the examination, you must compare elements of two texts – you might be asked about purpose and audience, language, presentational devices, the use made of facts and opinions or how successful the texts are.

You will be expected to:

- deal with *both* texts
- refer to the texts and *quote* to illustrate points
- make *direct comparisons*
- be *analytical* rather than descriptive: say *how* and *why* particular elements have been used and explain their effects.

Source text

Consider these extracts:

Sunderland footballer gives a fortune to the needy
Quintessential goodness!

By Samira Khan, social affairs correspondent

Recently, football's reputation has taken a battering. Players and fans have been under the spotlight, as 'the perfect game' has been beset by problems many thought had disappeared: hooliganism, violence and pitch invasions. But now a footballer has risen above all that. Niall Quinn of Sunderland has decided to give the money from his testimonial game – probably £1 million – to hospitals and to projects supporting children in underdeveloped countries.

All for good causes

Supporters will pay £20 each in May to watch Sunderland play the Republic of Ireland. Under normal circumstances, the money raised would go to Quinn, as a 'thank you' for his years in football.

Niall Quinn – a *real* footballing hero?

However, instead of pocketing the takings, he is giving them away. Some cash will go to local hospitals and the rest will help children abroad.

He was massively affected when visiting a children's hospital as a young player. The memory stayed. This is not his first gesture to help others less fortunate, but is one that will be long remembered.

Contrast

International Denis Wise, in contrast, was reported to have spent some money raised by his testimonial on Rolex watches for those who played… .

Source text

This is part of a leaflet:

Can you help?

As a charitable organisation working in this area, Help a Child has played a significant part in supporting social services, children's play schemes and those helping the homeless and dispossessed. We have, however, reached a point of crisis, and are begging you to offer either donations or your time to allow us to continue our work.

We have suffered:

- a 50% drop in financial income since the arrival of the National Lottery
- a 10% reduction in our council grant
- the loss of our base at Alverthorpe.

'Why do we need Help a Child?'
Well, Help a Child has existed for 15 years, and in that time we have managed to… .

A candidate's response

Asked to compare the **purpose** and **audience**, and **language** of the texts, a Grade D candidate began:

The first text is a newspaper article for newspaper readers. The second text is a leaflet that must be aimed at adults because they are the ones with time and money.

The first text uses some language to catch the reader's attention like 'fortune'. It must also be written for good readers, because it uses long words like 'Quintessential'. It also says people have been 'under the spotlight', which is a metaphor, because they have not really. The second text starts off with a question to get the reader's attention and then uses another one to link into what the leaflet is going to say next: 'Why do we need Help a Child?'.

The answer gives some detail from the text, but not much on purpose and audience.

Different kinds of reader

TASK 4

a. What kind of reader is the newspaper aimed at? Consider, very briefly, the visual impact and language used.

b. Who is the leaflet aimed at, and how do you know? Again, explain your decision with reference to the text.

c. What is the purpose of the article? What impression is it trying to create?

d. What is the purpose of the leaflet? This may seem obvious, but try to be as precise and detailed as you can. Remember to use your own words wherever possible.

Here, we have dealt with the texts separately, but when it comes to responding to a comparison question, you must make appropriate cross-references.

To move above Grade D, direct comparisons are necessary. It is not enough simply to write about one text on its own, then the next. Your points must be joined, using comparative vocabulary, if you wish to move into the A*– C Grades.

Comparative vocabulary is easy to use. You can connect points by using links such as:

- *on the other hand; however; yet;*
  Although the first text ..., the second...; in contrast; in comparison; but

similarly

- *Just as the first text..., so the second; In the same way that...,*
  similarly ..., and so on.

TASK 5

What words or phrases would you add between your answers to 4a and 4b, and 4c and 4d, to make the comparisons clear?

Clear comparison leads to a 'C' Grade. However, for the highest levels, you are expected to **analyse** each element – language, the use of fact and opinion, and so on – in greater detail. For instance, you might be able to compare more than one feature.

This is an extract from 'A' Grade comparison of language:

> When the writer says 'on weary wings', the alliteration of slow 'w's creates the effect of tiredness. This contrasts with the liveliness of the second text, where the short sentences build rapidly to a climax: 'She had won'. There is also a difference in the kind of vocabulary used by the writers... .

precise vocabulary ('alliteration') and the effect explained

technical feature, with textual evidence

clear and relevant comparison

developing further comparisons

EXAMINER'S TIP

Be cool. Be clear. Don't try to write about every linguistic feature in lengthy texts. This often produces lists of devices rather than analyses of them. Since the examiner wants to be convinced of your ability to analyse effectively, settle for commenting *precisely* on just three or four examples of language usage in each text.

TASK 6

Compare the language used in the two texts about charitable donations.

- Move beyond the 'D' Grade example by explaining exactly what effects are achieved, rather than just listing significant features.
- Remember that you must employ a comparative vocabulary to ensure good marks.

Extended practice

TASK 7

Read and compare the following texts.

In your answer, discuss:

- purpose and audience
- use of fact and opinion
- language
- presentation
- the success of the texts.

EXAMINER'S TIP

To clarify ideas, always deal with bullet points one at a time, including reference to both texts.

For example:

- purpose and audience in Text 1, then Text 2
- use of fact and opinion in Text 1, then Text 2

and so on.

Text 1: Newspaper article

The rat-a-tat-tat of a doorstepper's revenge

There were a couple of paragraphs in *The Sun* last Thursday that will have cheered the heart of anybody who has been called to the door bleary-eyed on a Sunday morning by a smartly dressed young man who wishes to talk at length about Jesus.

Jane White, of Peacehaven, East Sussex, was so fed up with Jehovah's Witnesses knocking at her door that she decided to exact an ingenious revenge. She found the nearest Kingdom Hall, where Jehovah's Witnesses worship, and waited until a service was in progress. Then she beat loudly on the door, waited for somebody to answer, and launched into a long lecture about Nirvana.

She kept up her talk for 20 minutes, immune to all appeals to go away. Eventually the congregation called the police. A spokesman for the Jehovah's Witnesses told *The Sun*: "People only have to say they do not want us to call and we won't return."

The technique has wide applications. Why stop at the Jehovah's Witnesses? Let's find out when the managing directors of double-glazing companies are just about to sit down for dinner so we can phone them up and ask if they're thinking of having new windows installed. Let's phone BT executives at inconvenient moments to see if they are taking advantage of the latest cheap-rate tariffs.

Jane White of Peacehaven, you don't know what you've started… .

The Sunday Times, 20 January 2002

Text 2: Featured letter from a newspaper

We could live in a haven of peace ... .

Dear Sir,
Last week, national newspapers took their opportunity to attack Jehovah's Witnesses. Readers were encouraged to sympathise with a woman who decided to take 'revenge' on Christians who had knocked on her door, by disturbing their worship. What a joker she is!

But police had to be called to remove her. And when you consider what happened, you must ask: What sort of country are we living in?

Jehovah's Witnesses hurt no one. They talk to people in the hope of saving souls. Is it wrong to care so much? It seems to me that there is a huge difference between knocking on a door to try to explain the mysteries of eternal salvation and wrecking a religious service. One action stems from love, the other from spite.

The congregation will have prayed for the soul of Jane White from Peacehaven, who disturbed them. Yet, how ironic that she should feel it necessary to break into their haven of peace, demonstrating the very attitudes that Jehovah's Witnesses would so much like to change.

I hope that she finds tranquillity in her life. Those who have already found God are the lucky ones.

Yours faithfully…
(Name and address supplied)

Jehovah's Witnesses at worship.

KEY SUMMARY

Aim to:

- use an appropriate vocabulary to describe devices in a text
- explain the effects produced by devices and analyse them rather than simply describe what is there
- make any comparisons direct and detailed, using comparative vocabulary.

Paper 1, Section B: Writing to argue, persuade, advise

Unit 5: **Planning a written response**

In this unit you will:

- follow a planning process for Section B questions
- practise completing stages of the process
- focus on the development of responses.

Answers to Section B questions require careful planning.

On the examination paper, you are advised to spend ten minutes preparing your ideas, before you begin to write your response.

EXAMINER'S TIP

A detailed plan = an improved structure = a better mark.

The planning process

All responses to Section B questions can be approached the same way, using four simple stages.

Stage 1: Identify the purpose and audience

To make sure you concentrate on *exactly* what the question demands, underline or highlight the most important words or phrases in the title.

For example: Write a letter to the Prime Minister, in which you offer advice on what the government should do to improve the quality of life in Great Britain.

Stage 2: Produce a spidergram of ideas

For example:

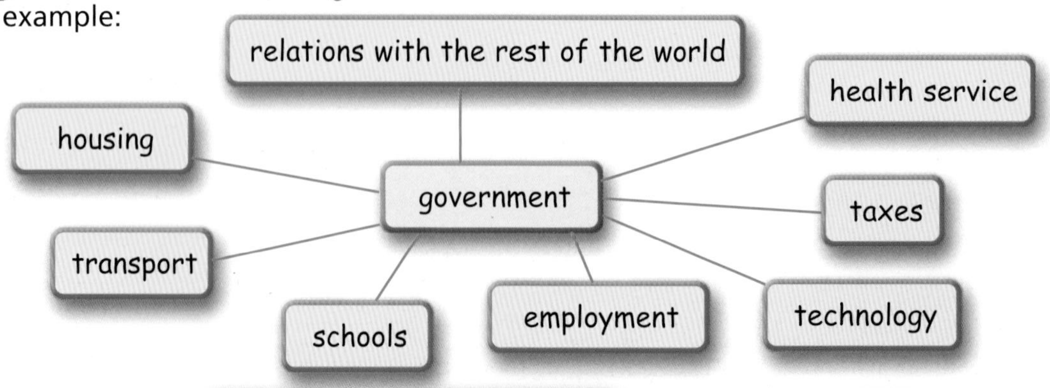

government
relations with the rest of the world
health service
housing
taxes
transport
technology
schools
employment

Where does it fit?

PAPER 1	PAPER 1	PAPER 2	PAPER 2
	✔		
SECTION A	SECTION B	SECTION A	SECTION B

Stage 3: Use your ideas to develop a detailed plan

You should:

- place your ideas into a logical sequence
- support each idea with additional notes, so that you know exactly what will be included in that section of your response.

For example:

1. **introduction**
2. **health service**
   - more GPs
   - swifter treatment
   - investment in hospitals
   - general availability of treatment (drugs, operations, post-operative care)
3. **schools**
   - improvement in buildings
   - books
   - recruitment of teachers
   - changes to school day
   - changes to school terms
   - subjects studied
4. **housing** ... .

TASK 1

Complete the detailed plan.

Stage 4: Add a palette of useful words and phrases

Produce a selection of:

- discourse markers, to link, develop or emphasise ideas
- phrases to use in your response.

This creates the equivalent of a painter's palette, into which you can dip as you write.

For example:

Discourse markers
however
what is more
nevertheless
in addition

Phrases
The most pressing need in the country today is... .

Incredibly, some public services are deteriorating ... .

TASK 2

Complete the palette, adding discourse markers and ideas of your own.

Developing writing responses for Paper 1

Organisation is the key to successful argument, persuasion and advice: the forms of writing tested in Section B of Paper 1.

If you have clear strategies to support your ideas, the writing process becomes simpler and more effective.

One approach for consideration is to develop your response at some point by using a sequence of three short paragraphs to build to a powerful point. Consider, for example, these paragraph openings, which might be used for:

1. Simple ordering – for emphasis and reinforcement

- One reason… .
- Another reason… .
- The main reason… . The most important reason… .

2. Countering or pre-empting an opposite viewpoint

- Some people think that… .
- Other people think that… . Despite this… . On the other hand… .
- Overall, most would accept that… .

3. Warnings and implications

- If people don't stop… . What some people do not realise is… .
- The disadvantage/problem/danger of this is… .
- The urgent need is to avoid… . The likely result of this will be… .

4. Drawing on extra support

- Recent research from the University of… .
- As my great great grandmother, who was 103 and nearly blind but could still drink my father under the table once said… .
- Twelve million people would not vote for this if… .

5.

Challenging the reader
- Have you ever asked yourself... ?
- Would you like it if... ?
- Can you honestly say that... ?

6.

Balancing conclusions
- There are two different principles involved here... .
- Whilst there is some truth in... . In the real world, perhaps... , but... .
- On balance, therefore, it seems fair to say... . After considering both sides of... .

TASK 3

Write three paragraphs of your letter to the Prime Minister, using one of these paragraph openings from three separate boxes.

After spending 5–10 minutes planning, take:
- 30 minutes to write your response, following your plan and concentrating on using language accurately and effectively
- 5 minutes to check your work.

EXAMINER'S TIP

Structuring ideas, so that each one develops effectively from what has gone before, leads to higher grades. For example, Grade A writing is 'coherently structured with fluently linked sentences and paragraphs'. Even if you choose not to include three short paragraphs in a response, the paragraph 'starters' offered will help you to link and develop ideas, and appropriate ones will be useful additions to your palette.

KEY SUMMARY

Use a planning process to improve the quality of your writing:
- Identify your purpose and audience.
- Produce a spidergram.
- Develop a detailed plan.
- Add a palette of useful words and phrases.
- Focus on how to begin your paragraphs effectively.

Unit 6: **Writing to argue**

In this unit you will:

- practise planning coherent arguments
- use a range of argumentative techniques
- focus on effective paragraphs, sentences and vocabulary
- concentrate on a range of texts, including newspaper and magazine articles and a letter.

What is writing to argue?

Its purpose is to convince the reader to accept one point of view rather than the alternative.

Good writing to argue:

→ is based upon logic
→ considers both sides of the argument
→ leads the reader to a definite conclusion.

High quality writing to argue also uses:

→ rhetoric
→ anecdote
→ examples
→ humour
→ emotive language
→ discourse markers to link ideas
→ varied and effective paragraphing.

45 MINUTES

Where does it fit?

PAPER 1	PAPER 1	PAPER 2	PAPER 2
	✔		
SECTION A	SECTION B	SECTION A	SECTION B

Likely topics

Section B questions will be related to the texts in Section A. However, you will be asked to argue about some **problem**, **situation**, or **idea** with which you are likely to be familiar, or about which you will be able to argue from a relatively informed viewpoint. The question is also likely to involve a precise **purpose** and **audience**.

For example:

1. **Write an article for a national newspaper in which you argue that 16 year olds should be allowed to drive.**
2. **Some worry that the Internet could prove 'a force for evil, rather than for good'. Write a letter to the Minister for Education, in which you argue that the Internet is either:**

   a. an excellent learning resource for schools, where its use should be developed

   or

   b. is over-rated as a learning support in schools.
3. **Write a welcome message for a new Health Centre's website in which you argue that it is important for all men over 40 to come in for a regular health check.**

TASK 1

Identify the purpose and audience in each question and then choose one and brainstorm the ideas you might use to respond.

Structures for arguments

You need:

- a clear introduction to the task – one that is interesting and grabs the attention of the reader
- logical progression through the sections of your argument – so that the ideas link effectively, the reader moves smoothly from one point to the next and any conclusions emerge, convincingly, from what has gone before
- an ending that rounds off your argument and prompts your reader to admit you have a point: and the examiner to award you a good mark!

A model text

This example shows how the writer has produced a clear and effective response to the task:

Write an article for a Sunday newspaper in which you argue that conventional warfare has had its day, and that nations need to find new ways to solve the world's problems.

Talks, not tanks, might save us ...

Millions of men fought in two world wars in the twentieth century, and civilisation as we know it was saved. The legacy of those conflicts, however, was not the hoped-for happy ending. Now, we are in a strange age: nuclear weapons exist, but we fear to use them; terrorism and biological warfare bypass boundaries and tanks; and any security provided by fighting troops seems insubstantial.

Of course, many argue that only by arming ourselves can we have any hope of survival. There is always a shadowy dictator lurking somewhere in a foreign state, they say, who rubs his hands together as he plans his sordid deeds against our democracy. Without a professional army, the latest planes and defence at sea, we would be like dominoes, knocked over in moments. Might is not right, they say, but is mighty necessary if you wish to defend yourself?

purpose

mature language

suitable tone for audience: challenging opening

discourse markers structure text

mature language

topic sentence introduces one side of argument

emotive image: powerful language encourages xenophobia

simile demonstrates lack of security

play on words with 'might' in previous sentence

short sentence implies doubt as does modal 'could'

opposite viewpoint introduced with rhetorical question

They could be correct. But, if so, how do countries like Switzerland, which spends so little on armaments, manage to survive and prosper?

Perhaps they have learnt from conflicts across the world where, at times, even the USA, with all its power, has been unable to crush relatively limited opposition. Perhaps they wish to rely on diplomacy rather than the threat posed by a nuclear submarine. And maybe the world is waking to the realisation that, like in Northern Ireland, differences can only be resolved through understanding, fairness and compromise.

repetition of 'perhaps' gives pattern and builds to a climax

the contrast with 'diplomacy' develops the point

example, could be developed further in a longer text

The grim reality is that modern enemies can be kept at bay only temporarily by a circle of soldiers. They will find a way through, round or under the protective cordon. The only way to be safe from them is to remove the friction and divisions which divide peoples. To be secure, we have to talk with our enemies, not try to shoot them.

summing up with a vivid image and a definite conclusion

TASK 2

Produce a detailed plan for an article that argues that warfare can be necessary.

Try to use similar features to those identified above.

- Come up with your key points (perhaps a maximum of ten).
- Put them in the sequence that is best for your argument (most important point first or last).
- Write down five or six key phrases or sentences you might use. For example:

  Warfare defends people's welfare.
  Are we really going to let other nations trample all over us?

Do not write the article. You are practising **the plan** only at this point.

Developing skills and techniques

Logical progression

When arguing, you should always keep in mind the opposite view – the one you are arguing against.

There are many different approaches you might use:

MODEL 1

Introduction

One side of the argument

The other side (dealt with in equal detail)

Ending

MODEL 2

Introduction

First point from one side

Alternative point

New point

Alternative point

New point

Alternative point

Final point

Alternative final point

Ending

MODEL 3

Introduction

Presentation of just one side of the argument, but always aware of the other point of view, using occasional references to it

Ending

MODEL 4

An extreme view
A moderate view
Your view

An extreme view
A moderate view
Your view

and so on ....

TASK 3

Structure the ideas from your Task 2 plan into a coherent argument, using one of the recommended models.

Priorities when writing to argue

- Be organised.
- Be interesting.
- Be aware that a reader might be sceptical or have the opposite view: be convincing!

Use of paragraphs

For examiners, varied paragraphing is a sign of higher quality writing, since paragraphs of different and appropriate length both interest the reader and help promote a desired response. They can, for instance, involve you in a topic, win you round to a point of view or take you by surprise.

At times, **longer paragraphs** might:
- set out one side of an argument
- give the detailed illustration of a particular point
- tell a relevant story.

On the other hand, **shorter paragraphs** might:
- make a brief but telling point
- challenge the reader, perhaps by using a rhetorical question
- change the emphasis in an argument.

EXAMINER'S TIP

Paragraphs give the examiner an immediate impression of your likely ability.

For example:
'Grade D' paragraphs are mechanical – the same length and are not linked well.
'Grade B' paragraphs are coherent, varied and used to create effects.

TASK 4

Look back at the plan you developed in response to Task 2. Extend it: decide how many paragraphs you will use and how each will begin.

Consider using discourse markers like:
- *One reason... . Another reason... .*
- *The most important point... .*
- *Some people believe... .*
- *Despite this... .*
- *On the other hand... .*
- *On balance, it seems fair to say... .*
- *Indeed... .*

TASK 5

The following extract, from a letter to a newspaper, employs an anecdote, to be followed by a short paragraph.

a. First, read the anecdote.

> Not all teenagers watch television. It is true that many apparently intelligent students return home from school, grab a packet of crisps and a can of Fanta, then mindlessly watch *Rugrats* for hours. However, others spend their time more profitably.
>
> One family I know does not possess a television, and when Laura has free time she reads, plays the oboe or paints. When she went to stay with her best friend for the weekend, she phoned her mother on Saturday, begging to be collected early. Laura simply could not cope with wall-to-wall and hour-to-hour cartoons and soap operas. She said her brain was stewing.

b. Now discuss the following short paragraphs and decide which one you would use. Say how they develop a point, change emphasis, and so on. Be precise when analysing their effect.

i. Laura is not an isolated example. Many youngsters have interests beyond television.

ii. Unfortunately, girls like Laura are few. Are not most homes permeated by the mind-numbing sagas of families in Weatherfield or Walford? There seems to be no escape.

iii. But, let's face it, most parents are happy to feed televised rubbish to children. Anything will do, so long as it keeps them quiet.

Use of sentences

Like paragraphs, effective sentences generally vary in length and content. Examine these two extracts from GCSE students.

It's silly to say that all children spend most of their lives watching television. We work hard at school, so why shouldn't we relax when we come home? If we do watch lots of programmes for younger kids, it isn't actually our fault, because there's nothing else on at that time. I don't see why we shouldn't do what our parents do – they seem to spend most evenings recovering in front of TV as well.

Emily – C Grade

I cannot help being lured to the sofa and our television. When I'm tired, they comfort me. They metaphorically soothe my furrowed brow. What is more, if I spend an evening with them, they don't cost me a fortune, unlike most of the girls I know. Anyway, it would seem a nonsense to have a magical box in the corner of the room, which can bring information and entertainment from around the world, and not make regular use of it.

Jamel – A Grade

TASK 6

a. Does Emily:
- use a satisfactory topic sentence?
- vary her sentences?
- link ideas effectively?

b. In what ways is Jamel's writing better?

Consider:
- his opening sentence
- how he uses humour
- how his sentences develop.

c. How do both writers show an understanding of another point of view they must counter?

Use of vocabulary

It is important that vocabulary is appropriate for the intended audience.

When Emily was writing, she employed a conversational style, using terms such as 'lots of'. She also abbreviated words in several instances, including the use of 'TV'.

Jamel, in contrast, wrote about 'the magical box in the corner of the room' and generally employed a wider vocabulary.

TASK 7

Imagine Jamel has been asked to develop Emily's paragraph, rephrasing her ideas and, where necessary, developing them.

Write Jamel's version, making sure you enrich the vocabulary and employ at least:

- one simile or metaphor
- one discourse marker.

This is the opening of an article by Barbara Ellen, a journalist who is arguing that middle age is the most difficult time in your life.

Sometimes I think that we all fear middle age more than old age, more than death. At least when you're old, you're old. At least when you're dead, you're dead. With middle age, nothing is definite – everything behind you is disappearing, and everything before you is just a frightening shape draped in fog. You're not yet old, and able to get away with walking down the street with a potty on your head, and you're also no longer young, and able to walk down the street wearing Vivienne Westwood (which more or less amounts to the same thing). Most pitifully, neither camp really wants you around – the former because you remind them of where they came from, the latter because you remind them of where they're going to end up. You're in no-man's land, running backwards and forwards, with both sides firing bullets at you.

The Observer Magazine

TASK 8

a. Decide which is the most significant word or phrase in each sentence. Write them down.
Seen together, what impression do they create?

When you are writing, always consider your words carefully. For example, which of these is more effective?:

- *She is quite convincing sometimes.*
- *She could convince you that the Queen lives on mushy peas.*

b. Was Barbara Ellen's opening paragraph effective? Why or why not?

Consider:

- the surprising nature of the topic sentence
- the way serious ideas are presented
- the language used.

Readers are sometimes more willing to accept points of view if they are not presented too seriously.

c. Noting in particular the final sentence, what is likely to be discussed in the remainder of the article?

The opening paragraph should give enough insight for you to be able to guess what might follow: if so, it is an effective introduction.

d. Write a final paragraph for the article.

Try to:

- link your writing with the opening paragraph and what you consider likely to have followed it
- imitate the writer's style
- round off your argument convincingly.

Some possible openings for your paragraph:

- *So, middle age, seen from every angle, is a dangerous time… .*
- *None of this, of course, will stop me growing middle aged. Eventually. Meanwhile… .*
- *Mock or shudder as you will, middle age is the battlefield we cannot avoid… .*

TASK 9

A first paragraph is presented below. Using the skills and techniques dealt with in this unit, complete the argument.

You may write your own opening paragraph if you wish, but make sure it is interesting.

Remember to:

- consider both sides of the argument
- develop your response logically
- vary paragraphs and sentences
- link ideas with discourse markers
- convince the reader: you might wish to use rhetoric, anecdote, examples, humour and emotive language
- end with a firm conclusion.

Also, of course, you will have to plan carefully before you begin.

Question:
Write an article for your school magazine in which you argue that work-related courses should replace GCSE work in Years 10 and 11 for any students who would prefer them.

Opening:
Across the country, tens of thousands of students in Year 11 hate school. Some are restless in lessons; others are more obviously disruptive. They have passed through an education that appears to have offered them nothing, and seems more intent on labelling them as failures than on preparing them properly for the remainder of their lives. They see no point in the academic studies they are forced to undertake. Surely it is time to reassess our priorities and begin to place the students and their needs at the centre of our system?

Possible sections to follow:

- Why academic courses do not suit all students.
- The effects of students' disenchantment on themselves and others at school.
- What happens after students leave school.
- How the curriculum could be changed to cater for the needs of all.
- The benefits of such changes for students, the school and the community.

Specimen exam questions

1. Should people who are severely ill be able to choose to die?
   Write a column for a national newspaper to **argue** for or against the idea.

2. Write an article for a television magazine, **arguing** that the more channels we have, the better.

3. Write a letter to the Prime Minister, in which you **argue** that action must be taken to ensure there is control of the Internet.

4. Write the script of a speech to be delivered to the rest of your year group, to **argue** that:
   - women still do not have the same opportunities as men

   or
   - the world has changed and women now have all the advantages.

One question will ask you to answer two or three of the purposes in the **argue/persuade/advise** group.

5. You are an agony aunt or uncle. Write a letter where you:
   a. give **advice** to a teenager about food hygiene and
   b. **persuade** them to eat a healthy diet.

6. Write an article for a tabloid newspaper where you aim to:
   - **argue** the case for more foreign aid
   - **persuade** the reader that foreign aid is a good idea for everybody's sake
   - **advise** the reader as to the best ways of helping the situation.

KEY SUMMARY

When writing to argue:

- plan carefully, bearing in mind that there are two sides to an argument
- vary sentences and paragraphs, linking ideas effectively
- use a variety of techniques to convince the reader.

Unit 7: **Writing to persuade**

In this unit you will:

- practise using persuasive techniques
- focus on:
  - how to open and develop persuasive responses
  - the use of anecdote, humour, rhetoric and emotive language
- deal with a range of texts, including an article by Germaine Greer, GCSE work and a variety of other extracts.

What is writing to persuade?
Its purpose is to convince the reader to agree with the writer.

Good writing to persuade:
→ emphasises one opinion
→ employs persuasive vocabulary and ideas throughout
→ leads the reader to make some choices.

High quality writing to persuade also uses:
→ anecdote
→ humour
→ rhetoric
→ emotive language.

45 MINUTES

Where does it fit?

PAPER 1	PAPER 1	PAPER 2	PAPER 2
	✔		
SECTION A	SECTION B	SECTION A	SECTION B

The art of persuasion

Although writing to persuade can be similar to writing to argue, there are usually differences. Argument weighs opinions against each other; persuasion can often be more emotional.

A: *Could I have some extra money, Mum? I know it means they'll repossess the gas cooker. But we all love sandwiches ... and I know I already owe you £307.57, but I want to propose a regular repayment scheme, which will benefit us all... .*

B: *Please, please can I have some money, Mum? I'll wash up for a week. I'll never ask for anything ever again. Please, Mum... .*

TASK 1

a. How are these children trying to get the money?

b. Who is likely to be more successful? Why?

Persuasive techniques

Weighing opinions (as you do in 'Writing to argue') can be vital when you have to persuade someone who might hold an alternative viewpoint.

For example: **Your local council said it would extend services for the elderly, but has now decided to concentrate on improving roads instead. Write an article for the local newspaper to persuade the council to change its mind.**

However, many other topics are less contentious; you might employ just **one viewpoint**:

Write an article for a newsletter, to persuade local residents to support a sponsored walk in aid of famine relief.

Likely topics

The questions on the examination paper are linked to the materials in Section A. As with writing to argue, you must address the particular **purpose** and **audience**, but should already have some knowledge of the topics.

TASK 2

You are trying to persuade your parent or guardian to let you have some money.

Make a list of the different ways you might try to persuade them.

A model text

Here, a top GCSE candidate aims to persuade the reader that Robin Hood's Bay is well worth a visit. He structures ideas successfully, writes accurately, uses techniques effectively and is imaginative.

This response uses language imaginatively to captivate the reader.

Topic sentence uses an oxymoron – contradiction in terms – to interest the reader ('new, old'), suggesting the experience is new to visitors but has been there for ages.

Ghostly press gang made real – 'you pause' is placed inside commas, making the reader, too, halt momentarily.

Robin Hood's Bay will offer you a new, old, quite unique experience. The walk from the cliffs to the beach is steep and cobbled. On the descent past the stone cottages, 'you pause', and can still hear the press gangs dragging men to the ships centuries ago. So little has changed. The old women in black who run the shop by the slipway have probably worked there for four hundred years, opposite the ale house, beside the waves. Only the voices of foreign tourists are a new addition.

When the tide recedes, boulders strewn with weed stretch out and away and as the bay opens before you, it entices you to walk, and to discover: for this is the dinosaur coast. Men hammer at rocks; wives investigate pools containing more than crabs; Steven and Cherry work their way through piles of stones, then scream loudly as they find fossils over 150 million years old. Parts of prehistoric squid and shellfish, solid now as stone, are just lying around.

Short sentence: simple and undeniable.

Humour.

The village attracts foreigners, so the opening point, that it is worth a visit, is re-emphasised.

The sentence stretches on like the beach, implying size and possibilities.

The beach seems busy with discovery through a complicated list supported by a brief anecdote.

The dinosaur coast, introduced at the start of the paragraph, seems rich in finds.

The subtle use of language: the verb seduces the reader, as the bay does the visitor.

A few miles away is Whitby, home of Dracula, the abbey, cluttered hillsides and steps, a harbour alive with seals, jumbled shops and the smell of fish and chips. This is not Blackpool or Brighton. The North Yorkshire coast is more basic and rawer than that. It is better.

So you should not visit Robin Hood's Bay for just a day. The area deserves more time and more consideration. You need to watch the stars over the sea and wind back up the hill in the dead silence of the traffic-free night. You need to feel the history heavy on you and relish a village that gives more than it takes. Then, you need to ask: would I prefer to be anywhere else? I know what my answer would be.

Whitby appears vibrant. Its description is squashed into one sentence.

A direct comparison.

A short, direct sentence again.

A logical conclusion.

Romance and magic is suggested.

A metaphor for the senses ('relish'): a sense of gain from a visit reinforced.

Alliteration makes history seem imposing.

A rhetorical question summarises writer's feelings.

TASK 3

a. Think of a place you love, it could be:
   - a holiday destination abroad
   - somewhere you have visited in the UK
   - somewhere local you know well.

b. Imagine you have to persuade others to visit it.

c. Write down a list of sentences you might use, employing some of the techniques above.

Developing skills and techniques

To persuade, you need:

- a well-structured plan
- well-connected sections
- an interesting opening and a compelling ending
- a range of persuasive techniques, which might include:
  - rhetoric
  - anecdote
  - humour
  - emotive language.

We will be dealing with these later in the unit.

Structure

Structure is always essential. Without it, the message is likely to be unclear.

A good structure:

- Introduces the subject and sets out your viewpoint.
- Develops your views, using examples.
- Produces an ending that sums up your feelings and relates back to your opening.

Openings

Your first paragraph, to introduce your subject, might start in one of these ways:

1. **Rhetorical challenge**
How many would have the temerity to go on national television and argue with Anne Robinson? Who would sleep soundly the night before engaging in a TV debate with Tony Blair or helping to interview Madonna? Quite simply, cameras intimidate us.

2. **Balanced explanation**
Battle lines are being drawn: supporters of *EastEnders* believe the programme should win every award available; whilst *Coronation Street* fanatics shake their heads and argue the case for the world's longest-running soap. However, both programmes have their strengths... .

3. **Exemplification: particular to general**
A broken man sits on the pavement. He could be any age: his hair is long and his face is thin. He says he has not eaten for two days. No one is helping him, and he will die soon. He is just one more statistic. People walk past and ignore him.

4. **Exemplification: general to particular**
'All the world's a stage.' Everywhere, people are acting a part and we cannot trust anything, no matter how obvious it seems. How do we know the rich are really happy? After all, who would want to suffer the life of Britney Spears?

TASK 4

Write four different opening paragraphs in response to the following task:

> **Write the text for a website that is trying to persuade teenagers to listen to classical music.**

Use different techniques:

- challenging
- explanatory
- using exemplification – particular to general
- using exemplification – general to particular.

EXAMINER'S TIP

When planning your persuasive response, consider different openings: your first idea is not always the best.

Developing an idea

As you organise your ideas, make them follow logically, so the reader understands your train of thought.

This is the opening of an article by women's rights supporter Germaine Greer. She is attempting to persuade her readers that there are many worthy women poets:

> *Every now and then I get a letter from someone who demands that I tell him why no female Shakespeare has emerged. He usually goes on to demonstrate to his own satisfaction that women are no good at anything and will never be any good at anything.*

TASK 5

a. Read the following topic sentences from other paragraphs in the article.

1. *There have been many more than 101 women poets in English.*
2. *Still, there is a real issue here and that is whether women have ever been or will ever be as creative as men.*
3. *And as for there being no female Shakespeare, the wonder is not that we do not have two Shakespeares but that we ever had one.*
4. *Phillips is a good poet, and capable of a kind of directness and energy not to be found in Cowley or Waller, the best of her male contemporaries.*

b. Decide which is likely to begin:

- the second paragraph
- the final paragraph
- a paragraph from the middle of the article
- the penultimate paragraph.

c. Give your reasons.

Enlivening the text

It is vital that you remain persuasive throughout your response.
This can be helped by the use of:

1. Anecdote

When you illustrate a point by including mention of something that really happened, it becomes much more accessible to the reader. Most people respond more readily to a story or happening than to a general idea.

Of course, this is not story writing, so the anecdote must be *brief* and *appropriate*.

Consider using anecdotes like this, from a sports magazine:

The Tour de France itself is not free from crashes. The television audience of millions watched three top riders spilling into the road, wheels buckling. Ambulances took the victims to hospital... .

TASK 6

Imagine you are planning a letter to persuade your Head of Year to organise regular social evenings for students in Years 10 and 11.

Write two anecdotes you might include, to show the evenings would be really valuable, illustrating:
- how some teenagers might otherwise spend their time
- the benefits of organised activities.

2. Humour

It is not easy to make people laugh. That is probably why so many comedies on television are written by the same successful people. However, if you include a sentence to make a reader smile and it fits with what you are saying, you can win readers to your viewpoint and gain credit in the examination.

For example, you might make readers laugh by using: exageration, the unexpected, sarcasm, and understatement.

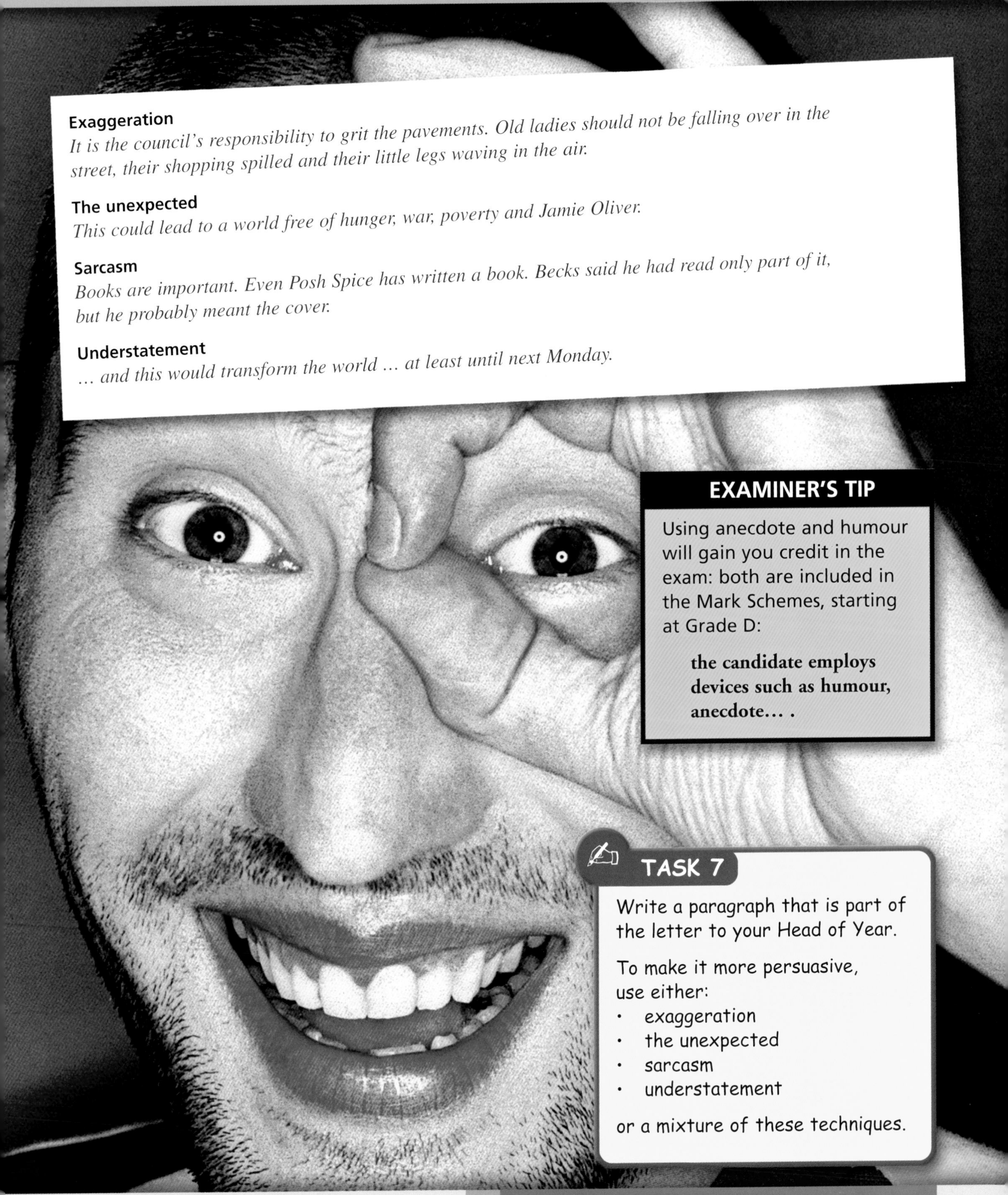

Exaggeration
It is the council's responsibility to grit the pavements. Old ladies should not be falling over in the street, their shopping spilled and their little legs waving in the air.

The unexpected
This could lead to a world free of hunger, war, poverty and Jamie Oliver.

Sarcasm
Books are important. Even Posh Spice has written a book. Becks said he had read only part of it, but he probably meant the cover.

Understatement
... and this would transform the world ... at least until next Monday.

EXAMINER'S TIP

Using anecdote and humour will gain you credit in the exam: both are included in the Mark Schemes, starting at Grade D:

> **the candidate employs devices such as humour, anecdote... .**

TASK 7

Write a paragraph that is part of the letter to your Head of Year.

To make it more persuasive, use either:

- exaggeration
- the unexpected
- sarcasm
- understatement

or a mixture of these techniques.

Developing skills (continued)

3. Rhetoric

This is 'elaborate language, which aims to persuade or impress'.

Rhetorical questions, in particular, help persuade your audience. Rather than expecting a reply, they make a definite point:

Rhetorical question	**Point**
Is this acceptable in the modern day?	*It is not acceptable.*
How many would admit to enjoying opera?	*Very few are likely to admit to enjoying opera.*
Could the situation get still worse?	*Possibly, it could.*

Such questions should be used sparingly, for maximum effect.

TASK 8

Write another paragraph of your letter.

This time, begin or end the paragraph with a rhetorical question, which might:

- surprise the reader

or

- make the reader think.

For example: *Would you want to spend every evening hanging around in the rain?*
Didn't you enjoy social events when you were younger?

Rhetorical statements

Many candidates in the examination recognise rhetorical questions, but fail to notice that there is rhetoric elsewhere. It might:

- be figurative – *He can be trusted to draw upon all the deep wells of memory and knowledge plumbed throughout his long life.*
- be exaggerated – *Like me, you must have read a thousand similar articles in your newspaper, and like me you must have found them all very unconvincing.*
- use repetition – *I loathe such behaviour; you loathe such behaviour; and, together, we must ensure that such behaviour plays no part in our society.*
- simply, be elaborate enough to impress and persuade the reader – *Under such tragic circumstances, it could have been no surprise to anyone when the young girl died.*

TASK 9

Write the final paragraph of your letter.

Include one or more rhetorical statements.

4. Emotive language

Emotive language touches the emotions.

It might:

- evoke pity – *She was drained and shaking.*
- deal with

  anger – *I witnessed a kind of barbarity it is hard to describe.*

  love – *His lips were soft as satin.*

  pride, nostalgia, injustice or shame – *She was proud of her daughter; I wish I was young again; It's so unfair; I feel terrible about it.*

EXAMINER'S TIP

If you concentrate on how to use emotive language, it will pay dividends in the examination. Like rhetoric, it is an important element in the mark scheme:

Grade F: candidates begin to use rhetorical devices, emotive language… .

Grade C: candidates should be able to use 'a more emotive style' and 'rhetorical questions'.

Grade A: candidates should use rhetoric, emotive language and other devices to 'adapt tone' and 'gain emphasis'.

This is part of a speech made by a prospective Member of Parliament, to persuade local voters to support her:

When I look around this community, I see so much that needs changing: housing, transport – the very quality of our life. I cannot walk past a child in rags or a teenager clearly wrecked by drugs without knowing that something must be done. I cannot sleep at night, knowing that something can be done. Why do we allow professional politicians, who know nothing about the poor and the sad and the ordinary people in our country, to sit on silk cushions at Westminster and decide how we – how you and I – will struggle to live and die?

TASK 10

a. Identify different elements of emotive language in the speech.

b. What are their intended emotional effects?

TASK 11

Write a paragraph about:
- the royal family

or
- British football supporters.

Use rhetoric and emotive language to arouse feelings of either:
- contempt

or
- patriotism.

Extended Practice

TASK 12

Title:
You are the editor of a 'Green' magazine.

Write an editorial, to persuade commuters to:
- use cars less often
- consider alternative means of transport.

Process:
1. Highlight the audience and purpose.
2. Brainstorm.
3. Put ideas into sequence.
4. Develop notes beneath each sub-heading.
5. List discourse markers, vocabulary and phrases you might wish to employ.
6. Begin to write.

Remember:
You might be more persuasive if you employ:
- anecdote
- humour
- rhetoric
- emotive language.

Consider whether an opening like this would suit your purpose:

> It is amazing how we, as commuters, continue to ignore the truth about what is happening to the environment. It is always someone else's problem, isn't it? It is up to the bloke down the road to consider the ozone layer, not us. Let the others give up their cars: why should we? After all, the bus keeps us waiting, and we get wet if we cycle or walk to work. Global warming doesn't seem so bad, so long as the car has air conditioning.

Also, use an effective ending – perhaps something like:

> So, we can make a difference. In fact, every time we leave the car at home, we are helping – and the ozone layer heaves a huge sigh of relief!

Specimen exam questions

1. Write a letter to **persuade** a top comedian to open a fundraising event at your school or college.

2. For a magazine supplement to a weekend newspaper, write an article **persuading** parents to be patient and understanding when dealing with teenagers, and to trust them more.

3. Write a newspaper article designed to **persuade** the government to spend more money on schools and hospitals, rather than on weapons and warfare.

4. An international conference for young people is being held in Paris. As a representative from Great Britain, write the text of a document to be handed out to other delegates, to **persuade** them that it is possible for people of all nationalities, races and religions to live together in harmony.

5. Write a letter **persuading** a cousin to spend less money on designer clothing.

6. For your school magazine, write an article to **persuade** the teachers to increase the number of extra-curricular activities available to students.

KEY SUMMARY

When writing to persuade you should:

- include different persuasive techniques in your plan, including anecdote, humour, rhetoric and emotive language
- use an interesting opening and definite conclusion
- be convincing.

Unit 8: **Writing to advise**

In this unit, you will:

- structure advice effectively
- focus on:
  - using an appropriate tone
  - using a variety of techniques to make advice effective
  - blending argument and persuasion when offering advice
- deal with a range of texts, including a letter, an editorial, students' writing, and an article from *The Independent on Sunday*.

What is writing to advise?

Most of us offer advice regularly: to friends, acquaintances … even football referees. However, the advice we shout at a sports event is unlike the advice you must structure and develop in a formal written situation.

In the examination, you might have to write for a magazine, a brochure, or to a public figure, like an MP. You will probably be expected to write in a formal way. You will aim to produce a response that is accurate and also original, so that it stands out and the examiner can reward you for your ideas, how they are organised and how you present them with sensitivity to the person you are advising.

Good writing to advise:

→ has a blend of argument and persuasion
→ is logical, so that the ideas are sequenced with each point connected to what has gone before
→ is convincing, to give confidence that the problem can be resolved.

High quality writing to advise also uses:

→ an appropriate tone
→ discourse markers
→ examples
→ a range of techniques, including:
  – use of the imperative tense
  – conditionals.

45 MINUTES

Where does it fit?

PAPER 1	PAPER 1	PAPER 2	PAPER 2
	✔		
SECTION A	SECTION B	SECTION A	SECTION B

Logic

Logic is a key concept. The *whole response* must make logical sense to the reader, which means that points develop from what has gone before. A reader should not wonder how one idea follows another: the sequence should clarify the meaning.

TASK 1

Put these ideas into a logical sequence:

- Arminah slipped in the crowd.
- High heels can be dangerous.
- Parcels went everywhere and an ambulance was called.
- Wise shoppers wear sensible footwear.
- Prince Charles was driving by and a crowd surged forward.
- Arminah is a perfect example of how we can suffer for fashion.
- One day, Arminah was shopping.

Each individual idea should extend from the previous one, whether the **logic** relies upon **facts**:

- *At high tide, the beach is covered by six feet of water. Make sure you do not get trapped when the tide comes in.*

or on **opinion**:

- *Your boyfriend has shifty eyes. You would be a fool to trust him.*

Discourse markers also play an important role. In these examples, they join the ideas to convince the reader:

Although I no longer felt sick, I held an empty bag over my mouth. Because the bag had a hole in the bottom, the situation became more unpleasant. My advice to you, therefore, would be to avoid such misfortunes by… .

TASK 2

Rewrite the information about Arminah, using at least three connective discourse markers to link ideas.

You may rephrase sentences when necessary.

You might need to use discourse markers like: however, because, when, as a result, consequently, therefore.

Model texts

The following texts display some of the elements that distinguish texts written to advise.

Letter to a friend

Dear Katie,

When I received your letter, I felt very concerned. It is clear that you need friends around you at a time like this; but since you feel so alone, I will do my best to offer some help, even if it is coming to you from such a distance.

Firstly, do not listen to what Jade and Sara have been saying. They are wrong. It is not true that you have to have the latest clothes to be attractive. Boys are not fooled by fashion: they are much more interested in what you are and how you behave. Yes, they like their girlfriends to look attractive, but there is more to attraction than just how you are dressed.

Secondly, don't put yourself down. I knew a girl once who felt she had nothing going for her at all, and allowed herself to become very depressed. Thank goodness she met a lad called Jimmy who rescued her from herself. She ended up marrying him. And we're still happy after thirteen years!

So, try to be more positive. Have faith in your own ideas, keep your head up and things will start to go right again. In fact, begin your new life by going to that party this weekend – you never know who you might meet.

Love...

appropriate tone for purpose and audience: personal voice

logical structure

persuasive techniques: conversational but very definite

clear advice: imperative used

counters other arguments

use of anecdote

touch of humour

positive ending

Newspaper editorial

The public knows that the government has failed to deliver on its promise to reduce hospital waiting lists and improve the National Health Service.

For anyone to claim that the problems stem from the actions of previous administrations is unacceptable. However, the fact that the government has at last pledged a proper cash investment is some sign that it has begun to see the light.

Urgent action is needed to relieve the sufferings of tens of thousands of people across the country. Serious investment in our hospitals and nursing services, properly funded by tax increases, was a policy long advocated by the Liberal Democrats, and it is sad that this government has taken so long to borrow the idea: but, hopefully, we will begin to move out of the darkness as it begins to implement the far-ranging, drastic and expensive reforms that we require.

As a society, we worry about old people needing hip replacements and those who need urgent cancer treatments. We care about the injured, sitting in A and E Departments for hours, waiting for attention. And so do the medical staff. Who can justify the current levels of trauma?

The government must give the money needed right now, and plan to avoid any such crises in the future.

Just as importantly, taxpayers must accept the financial burden, because, for any of us, it could be our light that goes out next.

purpose clearly established

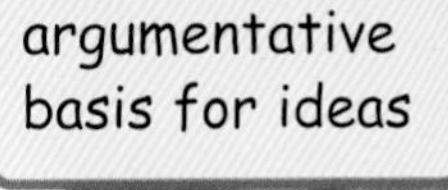

discourse marker to link ideas

advice

persuasive section

emotive examples

rhetoric

imperative tone

moves to logical conclusion

advice continues

effective ending through reference to recurring image

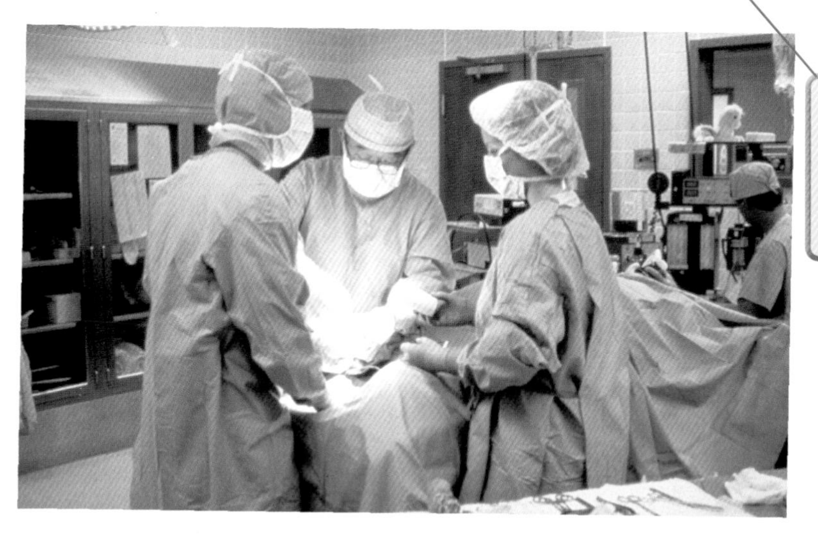

Developing skills and techniques

Effective structures

Writers use a range of structures to develop responses. Often, for example, the opening and ending are directly linked, giving a sense of 'rounding off' or completion:

Opening
Everyone in the city knows we must guard our homes against drug-crazed villains…

Ending
… so we have to follow police advice and lock our doors and windows: the man with the evil glint in his eye is probably 'casing' our houses right now.

Opening
How can you shake your head and deny what everyone else sees plainly?

Ending
To fail to respond to the advice you've been given would be foolish. In fact, if you continue to shake your head and do nothing, we'll be expecting sawdust to come out!

TASK 3

Below are two opening sentences from magazine articles offering advice. Write as many different endings as you can for each article, ensuring each version is clearly linked to the opening.

1. *As you sit, gazing at foreign currency the night before going on holiday, it can all seem very confusing.*
2. *More and more young men are spending as much on their appearance as do their girlfriends.*

Approaches

It is possible to present a situation *then* offer advice; or, to give advice at *each stage* in the writing.

Obviously, when we examine the behaviour of young revellers at New Year, there are a number of problems for communities to address … .

1. **Advice at end**

   Problems:
   Often, the first sign of trouble is… .
   What is more… .
   In addition… .

   Solutions:
   However, local residents need not despair. They can avoid difficult situations by employing a range of strategies.

2. **Advice interspersed**
   Problems and solutions mixed:
   When groups begin congregating and celebrating, householders could… .

   If noise is the main problem, then… .

Blending argument, persuasion and advice

Sometimes, we might simply set out a situation, then advise on how to deal with it. However, advice is usually based on an argument that is difficult to refute. Texts that advise, therefore, frequently follow a set pattern:

Argument → used to persuade the reader to accept → advice

This could be the central structure upon which the text is built, or might be used within individual paragraphs.

EXAMINER'S TIP

When scripts are marked, those with clear structures are usually most impressive. The time spent by students developing structural models will be rewarded by marks in the examination.

TASK 4

With a friend, read through this extract from a top candidate, and decide where the argument, persuasion and advice occur:

Some, pretending to be friends, will tell you that there are huge sums of money to be earned, consumables to be bought and bright sporty cars to drive. They will have you believe that the sensible ones wave a farewell to education as soon as possible and 'get a job, any job, mate'. And, if you believe them, it seems all those who don't move straight into education after their GCSEs never look back.

However, the truth can be very different, because we live in a world where qualifications count. How do you achieve promotion without certificates to say you are capable? Without the necessary courses, will you ever earn more money than your starting pay? Indeed, will you have a future at all?

No. Be wise. Spend time on A/S courses or a GNVQ. Make the most of yourself. Your life is too valuable to waste.

TASK 5

Use the pattern you have just looked at to advise a friend how to deal with 'problem parents'.

Developing skills

Formal and informal writing

It is important you adopt the correct register for your purpose and audience. For instance, a newspaper article that begins:

Don't wind up that big guy with the tattoos who's standing outside the ground every Saturday if you've any sense, pinhead.

is unlikely to be appropriate.

There will, however, be times when you are writing in a less formal style – perhaps when offering advice to an individual, such as in the advice about studying courses post-16 (see page 79). Remember that your response will be judged on vocabulary, sentence construction and paragraphing as well as ideas; so do not allow your style to become so conversational that you fail to do yourself justice.

TASK 6

This is the conclusion to an article in *The Independent on Sunday* about how best to avoid flu.

Read it, and decide:

- which features make it formal or informal
- whether the tone would persuade you to accept the advice, and why.

> Apart from a flu jab, says Dr Catti Moss, a GP, the best protection is a healthy diet, regular moderate exercise (athletes on rigorous regimes are more likely to get flu), and don't avoid crowds. "Research shows that doctors and teachers, who have lots of contact with people suffering from flu, are less likely to catch it, so don't shut yourself away."
>
> Ironically, the best protection of all is flu. "A bout will give you around seven years' immunity, and this 'active' immunity is stronger than that given by the jab," says Dr Moss. Focus on that as you sip your hot lemon.
>
> *Elizabeth Heathcote*

Techniques to advise

When writing to advise, you are likely to use the same techniques employed in writing to argue and to persuade: rhetoric, anecdote, humour and emotive language, for instance.

Examples are also likely to be important.
They can:

- show the negative side of situations –
  Top paid professional footballers need to behave responsibly, but these two did not. There is much we can learn from what happened.

- illustrate points positively –
  If Melanie emerged unharmed from her experience, so too can you.

- make points seem conclusive, when used cumulatively –
  Many have faced the disease and overcome it. On our street, Ken Jones, Sylvia Heath, Rohan Matthews and Brian Gosden have had treatment and been cleared to live a normal life – proving there is no reason for you to give up.

TASK 7

Imagine you are writing an article for the youth section of a local newspaper about how to resist someone who tempts you to experiment with drugs.

Write three sentences that you might include, each of which uses a brief example to:

a. make a negative point

b. make a positive point

c. build to a cumulative effect.

EXAMINER'S TIP

Just like anecdotes, any examples you use should be brief. If they are over-developed, the response can lose its direction.

Remember: you can ensure you are still responding to the title by re-reading it after every half page of writing.

The tone of advice

1. Imperatives

When offering advice, you can use an imperative approach, telling the reader what *should* be done.

Being assertive will present a sense of urgency, forcing the advice on the reader.

Use phrases like:
- *You must...*
- *You ought...*
- *You should... .*

or be even more direct:
- *Find a local group involved with pollution control. Do it today!*
- *Move away. Make a fresh start. It is the only way.*

2. More subtle approaches

Advice can also be presented more subtly. A reader might accept advice more readily if it is presented less aggressively.

When a lighter touch is needed, use phrases like:
- *You could...*
- *You might... .*

Many people are more willing to accept advice if they feel that the ultimate decision is their own. In such cases, rather than being assertive, tactful language is likely to have the most effect:
- *You may like to...*
- *It will already have occurred to you that...*
- *It might prove most convenient to... .*

When advice is not sought, it is best if it can be made appealing:
- *Teenagers often find the problem is less severe if they...*
- *What happens in other parts of Europe could serve as a blueprint for future developments here... .*

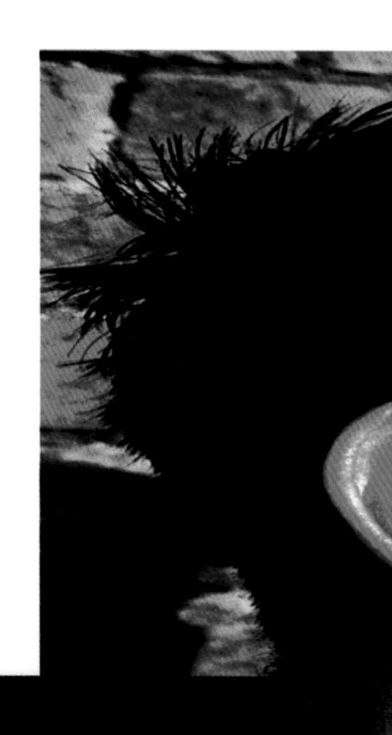

EXAMINER'S TIP

If you include occasional conditional phrases such as 'If this does not work, then...' or 'If this fails, you could...', you are showing you are aware that advice has to be adapted to circumstances, and is different from instruction.

TASK 8

a. Read this piece of advice:

There is no reason why you should have to put up with these hooligans who are making your life a misery. The solutions are simple: let the parents of the hooligans know that enough is enough, try to get your neighbours to support you, and contact the police. Of course, you must also take care to protect yourself against any revenge the vandals could take. Get yourself a large dog (preferably a Rottweiler); set up barbed wire around the house; and, if you can, dig a moat and fill it with sewage water. I honestly feel you will have no more trouble.

b. Rewrite the advice, making it less assertive..

3. Convincing touches

Being aware of the reader's needs can make advice much more convincing.
You can show respect for your audience by presenting:

- a range of options for the reader to choose from: *It seems to me that there are several ways this problem could be handled...*
- a clear explanation of what might happen if:
  - your advice is accepted: *If you follow this advice, I am certain that...*
  - your advice is rejected and another course of action put in its place: *On the other hand, to go down the opposite route could lead to tragedy. The first thing that will happen is...*
  - nothing is done: *Of course, you will be tempted to wait and simply see what happens. However, I fear that what you will find is... .*

TASK 9

Write a short article for the school magazine, advising students how to cope with bullies.

Use some of the techniques you have studied in this unit.

Extended practice

TASK 10

Plan and complete the response below, including:

- an appropriate range of persuasive techniques
- anecdote
- humour
- rhetoric
- examples
- a conclusion that links to the opening.

Title:

Your cousin has just been 'signed up' by one of the following:

- A professional football club.
- A top sports team.
- A record label.
- A modelling agency.

In future, they will be spending much of their time away from home, with a new lifestyle.

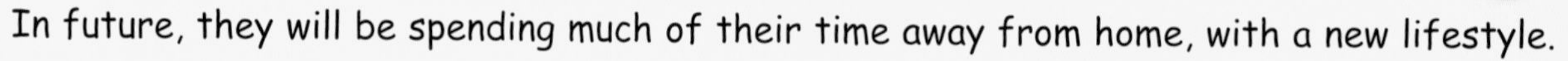

Write a letter to offer advice on how to cope with this new situation.

85 Marletts Drive
Stanningley
Worcestershire
W06 9KB

12 June 2002

Dear ______________

What excellent news! When Uncle Steve phoned to say what's happened, we were stunned!

You could include sections on:

- others who have been in a similar situation
- what your cousin might expect in his/her new life
- the problems of living away from home
- possible role models
- what the future might offer
- what is worth hanging on to from their present life.

Remember to structure your letter so that the ideas flow logically.

Specimen exam questions

1. Write an item to be included in a tourist brochure, to **advise** visitors how to get the most out of the area in which you live.

2. In the role of an 'Agony Aunt' or 'Agony Uncle' for a teenage magazine, offer **advice** to the writers of the following letters:
   - **a.** *I've just moved to a new area and need to find things to do with my evenings and at weekends. What do you suggest?*
   - **b.** *I don't follow fashion and don't want to dress like everyone else, but nobody seems to understand. What should I do?*

3. Write an article for a national newspaper in which you identify the main difficulties encountered by the physically disabled in our towns and cities and offer **advice** about how to improve the situation in the future.

4. Write a letter to a penfriend who lives abroad and intends to visit you, to **advise** him or her about how to cope with the British lifestyle.

5. Write a letter to a parent or older brother or sister:
   - **a.** **advising** them what they should wear if they come to your sixteenth birthday party
   - **b.** **persuading** them not to wear their usual clothes.

6. Write a letter to the BBC programme controllers to:
   - **a.** **advise** them how best to increase teenage audience figures
   - **b.** **persuade** them to drop some existing programmes and change the times of others.

KEY SUMMARY

When writing to advise:

- make sure you structure your writing logically
- illustrate your points, to be convincing
- use an appropriate tone
- employ a range of appropriate techniques.

Paper 2, Section A: Poems from different cultures and traditions

Unit 9: **Poems from different cultures and traditions**

In this unit you will:

- read ten poems from the *Anthology*
- explore each poem in depth
- update the special skills you need for this part of the exam
- practise your exam responses.

The poems you will study are:

'Island Man'	Grace Nichols
'Blessing'	Imtiaz Dharker
'Two Scavengers in a Truck, Two Beautiful People in a Mercedes'	Lawrence Ferlinghetti
'What Were They Like?'	Denise Levertov
from 'Search For My Tongue'	Sujata Bhatt
from 'Unrelated Incidents'	Tom Leonard
'Half-Caste'	John Agard
'Love After Love'	Derek Walcott
'This Room'	Imtiaz Dharker
'Not my Business'	Niyi Osundare

Examination requirements

The Anthology contains 16 poems from different cultures and traditions. The ten you study here will give you practice in the skills you need to apply to all of them.

What is special about poems from different cultures and traditions?

These poems are by modern writers from a range of cultures, but they all write in English. Some write about what they see in their local culture; others write about the differences between cultures they have experienced. The poets often choose not to use traditional verse forms, or traditionally 'poetic' language, preferring to experiment with forms and language that reflect the speech and life of their community. Many of the poems are meant to be performed to an audience, rather than read privately.

Where do poems from different cultures and traditions fit into the exam?

You will choose one of two tasks and will have around 45 minutes to write your response. You will have to compare poems.Your answer will count for 15% of your total mark in English.

Where does it fit?

How to use this unit

Each section contains a full copy of the poem being studied.

Under the heading 'Exploring the poem' you will find questions and tasks to help you develop your understanding and response.

These tasks will help you to:
- pick out the important themes in each poem
- focus on methods the poets use to convey their ideas.

Completing these tasks will:
- improve your understanding of each poem
- improve the way you show your understanding.

Five of the poems are followed by tasks that will develop your examination skills in meeting the Assessment Objectives. These skills are to:
- read with insight and engagement, making appropriate references to texts and developing and sustaining interpretations of them
- select material appropriate to your purpose, collate material from different sources, and make cross references
- understand and evaluate how writers use linguistic, structural and presentational devices to achieve their effects, and comment on ways language varies and changes.

There is more about these objectives in the relevant sections.

An eight-page section at the end of the unit covers revision and practice tasks.

EXAMINER'S TIP

Know your poems well, of course, but also know your assessment objectives, which are basically to:

- *interpret* the meanings of poems
- *make links* between the poems you study
- understand the *techniques* poets use to convey their ideas.

Island Man

(for a Caribbean island man in London who still wakes up to the sound of the sea)

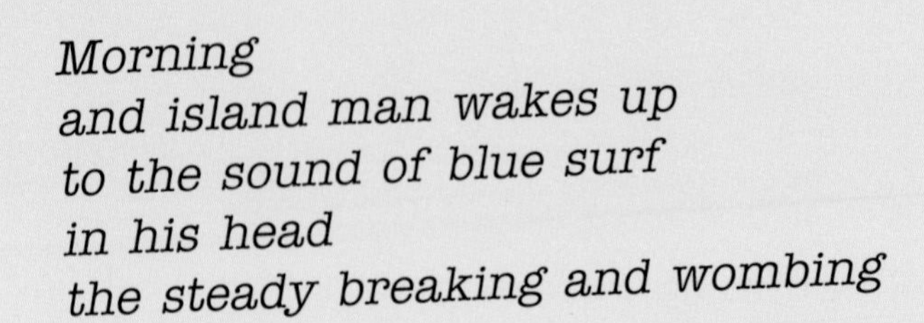

Morning
and island man wakes up
to the sound of blue surf
in his head
5 the steady breaking and wombing

wild seabirds
and fishermen pushing out to sea
the sun surfacing defiantly
from the east
10 of his small emerald island
he always comes back groggily groggily

Comes back to sands
of a grey metallic soar
to surge of wheels
15 to dull North Circular roar

muffling muffling
his crumpled pillow waves
island man heaves himself

Another London day

Grace Nichols

Exploring the poem

On the surface, 'Island Man' is a simple poem; a man is waking up in London, and he remembers… . Well, what does he remember?

Ideas and feelings

a. Waking up can be pleasant or unpleasant. We can feel refreshed or still tired. What makes this man's waking up seem pleasant?

b. Sometimes, when we first wake, we are not sure if we are fully awake or still half asleep. What suggests that the pleasant waking feeling in stanza 1 may be more to do with dreaming than real life?

c. What, in stanza 2, makes the recalled island scene seem attractive and unlike a city scene?

d. How are the colours and sounds of London linked to, but made different from, the island colours and sounds in stanza 3?

Language

a. How are repetitions used to suggest that real life may lack the vividness or clarity of memory or imagination?

b. How does the writer suggest that the noise of London begins to dominate the sounds that filled his bedtime? Mention a metaphor, onomatopoeia and the rhyme.

c. Which one word suggests the effort required to leave the imagined environment and get on with the London day?

d. Which of these statements do you think true: the first, the second or both?

- The poem is called 'Island Man' because the man comes from an island.
- The poem is called 'Island Man' because he is surrounded by a sea of city noise and bustle.

Structure

Grace Nichols has presented her poem in an unusual way.

a. How are the layout and punctuation different from what we might normally expect? What different effects do you think she was trying to achieve with her unusual presentation?

Developing skills and techniques

Assessment Objective

You need to *read with insight and engagement.*

When we probe for the meanings of particular words and phrases, we may suggest several possible meanings, but some may be more convincing than others.

'Engagement' means connecting with a text, feeling it says something to you. It is also what makes a reader want to keep probing for meaning. 'Insight' is what makes a reader see beyond the obvious and search out meaning.

Here are some comments made about 'Island Man'.

- It seems that the 'sound of blue surf' reminds the man of his washing machine.
- I think the 'wild seabirds' contrast with the feeling the man has of being trapped.
- Obviously, a lion has escaped on to the North Circular road.
- The repetition of 'groggily' emphasises the man's unwillingness to wake up.
- The ending of the poem, I feel, suggests the monotony of everyday life.

All these comments show engagement. Three of them suggest insight.

- Which two comments do not seem to fit the poem?
- Explain why the reader may have made them.

Now look at these comments about the use of the word 'wombing'.

- It rhymes with 'booming' and reminds us of the sound of the surf.
- It suggests the man was born into a life close to the sea.
- It indicates the difficulty the man is having being 'born' into a new day.

How a candidate might put these together:

The word 'wombing' suggests that the man was born into a life close to the sea. Its rhyme with 'booming' reminds us that the sound of the surf is what the man may hear in his dreams. It also indicates that he is unwilling to be 'born' day after day into a grey London morning.

EXAMINER'S TIP

Show that you know that words can mean different things to different people by using 'suggests', 'indicates', 'may mean', 'could mean' or 'perhaps' rather than 'says' or 'means'.

TASK

a. Make three comments about the phrase *'his small emerald island'* that show you are reading with insight and engagement.

b. Put your comments together into a short paragraph like the one about 'wombing'.

Extended practice

Focusing on the task

Comments about poems can be about ideas or language or what you think about them, but they need to focus on the task you are given.

You may have made the following reasonable comments about 'Island Man'.

- The colours of the Caribbean are attractive.
- London is associated with unattractive colours.

In response to the following task:

a. Discuss the ways in which a poet explores the contrasts between cultures.

You need to link any statements to the key words in it. The key words are 'the ways', meaning the techniques or methods. This means close reference to the use of language, so you may write something like this:

> Grace Nichols contrasts the 'blue surf' of the Caribbean with the 'grey metallic' ugliness of London. The contrast is emphasised by her use of the word 'emerald' to describe the man's island home. This suggests something precious and beautiful that has been lost in the new country.

In response to this task:

b. Write about the ways a poet expresses his or her love of a culture.

You would use your ideas about colours and bring in others like:

- The sounds of the island are appealing.

> Grace Nichols expresses her love of the Caribbean by writing about its bright colours like the 'blue' of the surf and the 'emerald' of the man's island. The use of the word 'emerald' indicates something precious that should be treasured. The sounds of the sea are 'steady' and regular and seem to match the relaxed rhythms of everyday life … .

FINAL TASK: CULTURAL DIFFERENCE

How does 'Island Man' explore the problems of cultural difference?

a. Make comments showing insight and engagement that focus on the task.

b. Organise your comments into a paragraph plan.

c. Use the extracts above as examples of how to help you express your ideas.

Blessing

The skin cracks like a pod.
There is never enough water.

Imagine the drip of it,
the small splash, echo
5 in a tin mug,
the voice of a kindly god.

Sometimes, the sudden rush
of fortune. The municipal pipe bursts,
silver crashes to the ground
10 and the flow has found
a roar of tongues. From the huts,
a congregation: every man woman
child for streets around
butts in, with pots,
15 brass, copper, aluminium,
plastic buckets,
frantic hands,

and naked children
screaming in the liquid sun,
20 their highlights polished to perfection,
flashing light,
as the blessing sings
over their small bones.

Imtiaz Dharker

Exploring the poem

Many of the things we have in our lives we take for granted. We only ever miss them if they are not there, or if they don't work. 'Blessing' makes us think again.

Different lives

a. Think about a typical day in your own life. Write about some of the things you rely on without ever considering them.

Now look again at the first stanza of the poem.

b. What is missing and how does it make people feel?

c. How would you feel if something essential to your own daily life was missing?

Impressions and moods

In the second stanza we are asked to imagine the sound of water.

a. Which four words draw our attention to sound?

b. Explain the metaphor that illustrates the reaction of the poet to the little water there is.

c. How does the poet create the impression that people are poor?

The mood of the poem changes in the third stanza.

d. What is the event that causes the change in mood?

e. Choose five words that convey the excitement of the scene.

f. How does enjambment add to the effect?

g. Which word does the poet use to show the high value of water?

Divinity, children and water

The word 'divinity' means 'Godliness'.

a. What is given God-like status or is worshipped in most European cultures?

b. What makes something a 'divinity' in this poem? Focus on the language used.

At the end of the poem, small children are playing.

c. What is there to suggest the children are poor?

d. How do they react to the water?

FINAL TASK: YOUR OWN REACTION

The poem can be seen as sad, joyful and full of messages about life.

Write about how the poem can be read in these different ways.

Two Scavengers in a Truck, Two Beautiful People in a Mercedes

At the stoplight waiting for the light
nine a.m. downtown San Francisco
a bright yellow garbage truck
with two garbagemen in red plastic blazers
5 *standing on the back stoop*
one on each side hanging on
and looking down into
an elegant open Mercedes
with an elegant couple in it

10 *The man*
in a hip three-piece linen suit
with shoulder-length blond hair & sunglasses
The young blond woman so casually coifed
with a short skirt and colored stockings
15 *on the way to his architect's office*

And the two scavengers up since four a.m.
grungy from their route
on the way home
The older of the two with grey iron hair
20 *and hunched back*
looking down like some
gargoyle Quasimodo
And the younger of the two
also with sunglasses & long hair
25 *about the same age as the Mercedes driver*

And both scavengers gazing down
as from a great distance
at the cool couple
as if they were watching some odorless TV ad
30 *in which everything is always possible*

And the very red light for an instant
holding all four close together
as if anything at all were possible
between them
35 *across that small gulf*
in the high seas
of this democracy

Lawrence Ferlinghetti

Exploring the poem

We often judge people on appearances. Think about stereotypes – the way we expect particular nationalities to look, or the behaviour we expect from particular professions. Perhaps, for example, we even expect 'posh' speech from people in pinstripe suits, or the opposite from builders. Such expectations are often unfair, but the judgements are hard to resist.

Appearance

a. In the poem, the two couples are presented to us in different ways.
Look for details that describe:
- the colours associated with the two couples
- their physical appearance, including their hair
- the way the couples are dressed.

b. Note down any similarities between the driver of the Mercedes and the younger garbage man. What reasons might Lawrence Ferlinghetti have had for making them similar in appearance?

American society

There may be other things that the writer wishes to say. The 'American dream' is an expression used to describe the belief of many people that America is a land of unlimited opportunity. It could be said that America has always advertised itself as a place where anyone can become happy and rich. Yet:

a. How do the comparisons in the poem's title emphasise divisions?
b. What is different about the modes of transport used by each pair?
c. Can you explain how the different ways of travelling might be seen as metaphors?
d. What do the differences between the couples suggest about American society?

Discuss with a partner how the idea of advertising is used in the poem.
e. What hope do you think is being offered to the garbage men?
f. What do you think is the poet's attitude towards the hope being offered?

Photographic impressions

The poem is structured like a series of snapshots taken over a very short period.
a. How does the presentation of the poem support this impression?
b. What is the approximate timescale of the events in the poem?
c. Is it important that the contact between the couples is so brief?
d. Why might the poet see himself as a kind of photographer?

Assessment Objective
You need to *comment on ways language varies and changes.*

The following short extracts are all from other poems in the *Anthology*.

- *Another London day* — 'Island Man'
- *yooz doant no thi trooth* — from 'Unrelated Incidents'
- *Sir, laughter is bitter to the burned mouth* — 'What Were They Like?'
- *explain yuself* — 'Half-Caste'
- *the bud opens, the bud opens in my mouth* — from 'Search For My Tongue'

a. Explain how language is being used in at least three of these. One is done for you.

> The phrase 'the bud opens' is repeated as if the poet can hardly believe what is happening. The language celebrates the 'flowering' of Sujata Bhatt's mother tongue. Using a dramatic metaphor like this is a way of conveying the delight the poet feels.

The language in Lawrence Ferlinghetti's poem is generally straightforward and uncomplicated.

For example: *'a bright yellow garbage truck with two garbagemen in red plastic blazers'* is clear and simple language – or **prosaic**, meaning that it looks like straightforward descriptive prose, which relies heavily on adjectives.

b. Why do you think Ferlinghetti chose to write most of the poem like this?

c. Why is the only simile so effective?

d. What effect does Ferlinghetti achieve by using fragments of language rather than complete sentences, properly punctuated?

e. Sometimes Ferlinghetti uses language that is not quite so clear and simple.

Read these descriptions of the couple in the Mercedes.
'The man in a hip three-piece linen suit… .'
'The young blond woman so casually coifed… .'
'The cool couple… .'

Try to imagine the way the poet would say the words 'hip', 'casually' and 'cool'. What do these words suggest about Ferlinghetti's attitude to the couple?

The last three lines

Read the final three lines of the poem. The language suddenly becomes more 'poetic'.

f. What point do you think Ferlinghetti is making in the last stanza?

g. Can you explain *how* the language becomes more poetic at this stage?

h. Can you say *why* you think Lawrence Ferlinghetti chose to make this point in poetic language?

Extended practice

Writing about language

If you were writing about how Lawrence Ferlinghetti uses language to help him express his ideas, you could include the following points about 'Two Scavengers in a Truck':

- Fragmented language suggests a series of 'photographic' impressions.
- Lack of punctuation creates an informal series of impressions.
- Language is generally simple and clear, to reflect a straightforward situation.
- Sometimes language is used to sneer at the wealthy couple.
- Poetic language at the end shows the poet's disbelieving attitude towards the dream of equal opportunity.

Extract from an A Grade response

Lawrence Ferlinghetti believes that Americans of different classes and backgrounds are more divided than united. There are cultural barriers that separate people despite the fact that advertisements pretend anything is possible and all are equal. As a consequence of this separation, it is a rare occurrence to see people as different as those in the poem in close proximity to each other. The poet 'captures' the moment at the traffic lights in a series of 'snapshots' or impressions. The snippets of language suggest a camera rapidly recording a set of images. We can 'see' the snapshots of the 'bright yellow garbage truck' being rapidly replaced with one of the 'elegant open Mercedes' and then the 'young blond woman'. The lack of punctuation in the poem reinforces this impression. We read the poem as a set of connected images rather than as a narrative that tells us a story.

This long paragraph:

- shows how Ferlinghetti uses language to create a set of impressions
- explains why this use of language supports his ideas about social divisions
- makes specific reference to language use.

FINAL TASK

a. Now complete the response on Lawrence Ferlinghetti's language use.

- Use the information you wrote about on the previous page.
- Quote to support what you are saying.
- Structure ideas into sensible paragraphs, for example:
  one paragraph on the garbage men
  one paragraph on the couple, and so on.

What Were They Like?

The Vietnam War was one of the most important military conflicts of the Twentieth Century. As well as films such as *Platoon*, many poems and prose works were written about it and the people involved.

Some details:

- The war lasted from 1959 to 1975.
- Communist North Vietnam was fighting South Vietnam.
- Fearing the growth of Communism, the US supported the South for the last ten years.
- 543 000 American troops were there at the height of the conflict.
- The war involved ferocious jungle fighting, intense air strikes and civilian casualties.
- 3–4 million Vietnamese died.
- 58 000 Americans died, and anti-war protests at home eventually contributed to the American withdrawal and defeat.

Pre-reading

Before you read the poem on the facing page, find out further information about the war. For example, where is Vietnam? What sort of climate does it have?

What Were They Like?

1) Did the people of Viet Nam
   use lanterns of stone?
2) Did they hold ceremonies
   to reverence the opening of buds?
3) Were they inclined to quiet laughter? 5
4) Did they use bone and ivory,
   jade and silver, for ornament?
5) Had they an epic poem?
6) Did they distinguish between speech and singing?

1) Sir, their light hearts turned to stone. 10
   It is not remembered whether in gardens
   stone lanterns illumined pleasant ways.
2) Perhaps they gathered once to delight in blossom,
   but after the children were killed
   there were no more buds) 15
3) Sir, laughter is bitter to the burned mouth.
4) A dream ago, perhaps. Ornament is for joy.
   All the bones were charred.
5) It is not remembered. Remember,
   most were peasants; their life 20
   was in rice and bamboo.
   When peaceful clouds were reflected in the paddies
   and the water buffalo stepped surely along terraces,
   maybe fathers told their sons old tales.
   When bombs smashed those mirrors 25
   there was time only to scream.
6) There is an echo yet
   of their speech which was like a song.
   It was reported their singing resembled
   the flight of moths in moonlight. 30
   Who can say? It is silent now.

Denise Levertov

Explaining the War

Responses

a. Different people will respond in different ways to the photographs of the war on page 100. Write briefly about how you would respond to these images if you were:
- a North Vietnamese villager
- an American soldier told to justify the war
- an American peace protestor.

b. Now imagine you were:
- an American newspaper journalist covering the war
- a North Vietnamese journalist covering the war.

If you had to choose one of these images for publication, which one would you select? Explain the reasons for your choice.

Asking the right questions

Now imagine you are an anti-war journalist. You have been given permission to ask three questions of the American military about the war. Write down the three questions you would ask. Explain why you would choose to ask these questions.

Here are some questions that are asked about the war in the poem 'What Were They Like?'
- *'Did the people of Viet Nam use lanterns of stone?'*
- *'Were they inclined to quiet laughter?'*
- *'Did they use bone and ivory, jade and silver, for ornament?'*

Discuss with a partner:

a. How do these questions differ from the ones you have asked?
b. Who would ask questions like these?
c. Why would anyone choose to ask these kinds of questions?
d. What answer might one of the following give to questions like these?
- a soldier
- a politician
- a peasant farmer

Giving the 'right' answers

Here is the answer given to the first question from the poem.
- *'Sir, their light hearts turned to stone.*
  It is not remembered whether in gardens
  stone lanterns illumined pleasant ways.'

a. What clue do we have about the identity of the speaker?
b. Why might the speaker have used the passive voice to answer the question?
c. How is the speaker's answer different from what you might expect?

Exploring the poem

Assessment Objective

You need to make *appropriate references to texts and develop and sustain interpretations of them.*

'What Were They Like?' can be interpreted as a poem that:

- attacks American politicians and soldiers for what they did in the Vietnam War
- asks awkward questions that make military logic seem irrelevant
- explores the guilt felt by the people responsible for the fighting
- celebrates the culture that the war destroyed.

Extract from a candidate's response

What you write about the poem should sustain some or all of these interpretations. This response is confused and is unlikely to reach C standard.

> The poet asks questions that are silly, irrelevant and naïve. They are questions that would not normally be asked, yet they seem more important than most journalistic questions. Vietnamese culture is presented as a simple one not worth saving. It is less sophisticated and less attractive than modern Western cultures. The poet believes that Vietnamese life before the war was characterised by humane and rich relationships.

a. This writer is not consistent in what he or she says. However, find the two sentences that do sustain the general interpretation.

You also need to make *appropriate references* that will support your interpretation.

b. Which questions would you choose to support the two sentences above that you identified?

c. What would you quote from the poem to support the following interpretations?

- The bombings were brutal and sudden.
- The second speaker feels guilty.
- Vietnam has been completely destroyed.

Explain your choices.

FINAL TASK

How has Denise Levertov used language and structure to promote her message?

Comment on features such as:

- the contrasts in moods
- enjambments, metaphors, the simile, alliteration, and so on
- the ending of the poem.

from 'Search For My Tongue'

You ask me what I mean
by saying I have lost my tongue.
I ask you, what would you do
if you had two tongues in your mouth,
5 *and lost the first one, the mother tongue,*
and could not really know the other,
the foreign tongue.
You could not use them both together
even if you thought that way.
10 *And if you lived in a place you had to*
speak a foreign tongue,
your mother tongue would rot,
rot and die in your mouth
until you had to spit it out.
15 *I thought I spit it out*
but overnight while I dream,

મને હતું કે આખ્ખી જીભ આખ્ખી ભાષા,
(munay hutoo kay aakhee jeebh aakhee bhasha)
મેં થૂંકી નાખી છે.
20 *(may thoonky nakhi chay)*
પરંતુ રાત્રે સ્વપ્નામાં મારી ભાષા પાછી આવે છે.
(parantoo rattray svupnama mari bhasha pachi aavay chay)
ફુલની જેમ મારી ભાષા મારી જીભ
(foolnee jaim mari bhasha mari jeebh)
25 **મોઢામાં ખીલે છે.**
(modhama kheelay chay)
ફળની જેમ મારી ભાષા મારી જીભ
(fullnee jaim mari bhasha mari jeebh)
મોઢામાં પાકે છે.
30 *(modhama pakay chay)*

it grows back, a stump of a shoot
grows longer, grows moist, grows strong veins,
it ties the other tongue in knots,
the bud opens, the bud opens in my mouth,
35 *it pushes the other tongue aside.*
Everytime I think I've forgotten,
I think I've lost the mother tongue,
it blossoms out of my mouth.

Sujata Bhatt

Exploring the poem

You are going to use a slightly different approach to this poem. Rather than discuss issues, or work around the poem, you are going to try to respond to some very direct questions.

Read the first 14 lines again.

a. What do you understand by the expression 'mother tongue'?
b. What does the poet mean by saying some people have 'two tongues'?
c. In what ways could it be an advantage to have 'two tongues'?
d. In what ways could it be a problem to have 'two tongues'?

Read lines 12 to 15.

e. List three powerful verbs used in these lines. Which of these are repeated?
f. What emotions are revealed by this choice of verbs?

Read lines 17 to 30.

g. Why do you think the poet chose to write these lines in Gujarati?
h. Why might she have decided not to translate them into English?

Read from line 31 to the end of the poem.

i. One verb is repeated four times and one phrase is repeated twice. Why do you think the poet uses these repetitions?
j. List five words that remind us of plants. Do you think the poet had a purpose in reminding us of plants?
k. How have the poet's feelings changed since the beginning of the poem?

A candidate's response

Working in this way can lead you to some very clear responses, such as the ones below.

The poet begins in a conversational style.
She is afraid of losing her mother tongue.
Phrases are repeated.
The poet uses the metaphor of a growing plant.
She is proud of the strength of her mother tongue.

However, you need to put other ideas down in a 'connected' way. Find evidence from the poem to support each statement then explain it in more detail. The first one is done for you.

The poet begins in a conversational style by using phrases such as 'You ask me' and 'I ask you'. She may have done this to remind us of the importance of spoken communication between people. It seems as if she is having difficulty making the other person understand her problems.

Language, structure and presentation

Assessment Objective
You need to show that you can *understand and evaluate how writers use linguistic, structural and presentational devices to achieve their effects.*

EXAMINER'S TIP

Linguistic devices are anything relating to a poet's special use of language.
Structural devices refer to the way a poem is organised into sentences and stanzas.
Presentational devices refer to the visual appearance of a poem or a part of a poem.

These devices are used by poets to help them emphasise the messages of their poems.

Sujata Bhatt could have written:
'I find it difficult to cope with being bilingual in a foreign country.'

Instead she writes:
'I ask you, what would you do if you had two tongues in your mouth... .'

a. How is language used effectively in this line?
b. How does her choice of language improve on the statement above it?

Sujata Bhatt divides her poem up into three clear sections.
c. How does this structure help the reader to understand her ideas and feelings?

Sujata Bhatt uses an unusual presentational device.
d. Identify the device and comment on its effectiveness.

Read the following sentence.
Sujata Bhatt uses the metaphor of a plant.

A linguistic device (the metaphor) has been identified but there is no comment on its effect. The following passage identifies the device and explains the effect it has on the reader.

> Sujata Bhatt uses the metaphor of a plant. This is an effective metaphor because it suggests something living and growing. The plant is associated with the beauty of the poet's language as it 'blossoms' from her mouth.

e. Read lines 12 to 15. How does the poet use language in an effective way in these lines?

Extended practice

Planning a poetry response

Go through the following stages before you begin to write: they will help you structure your ideas and prepare for the examination.

Stage 1: Read the task carefully and underline the important words.
Example: Write about the way that three poets express the difficulties of being in a minority.

Stage 2: Decide which poems you are going to write about.
First example: 'Search For My Tongue'.

Stage 3: Note down the points you are going to make and the evidence you are going to use.
Example:

Points	**Evidence**
People don't understand her	*conversation at beginning of poem*
Pain at losing own language	*tongue 'rots' and 'dies'*
Loves her dying language	*dreams in Gujarati*
Wants others to feel her sense of exclusion	*uses Gujarati script*
Needs to fight to keep her language	*image of tongues in conflict*
Overcomes difficulties	*image of tongue as powerful plant*

Stage 4: Putting it all together.

- When you are writing, points and evidence should be linked together.
  Example:

> The poet uses English because she lives in a country where it is the majority language and her mother tongue is rarely used, which means it may be gradually forgotten. This causes the poet great pain and suffering, since her own language is crucial to her identity. She refers to her fear that an unused language will 'rot and die' in its speaker's mouth. Her choice of such emotive words reminds us of corruption in nature. It emphasises how, if they are not looked after, both plants and languages can be lost.

point

quotation evidence

explanation

Stage 5: Note down points and evidence for the other poems you have chosen.

FINAL TASK

Now write a response to the task.

- Use your plan as you write.
- Remember to make a point, quote, then explain.

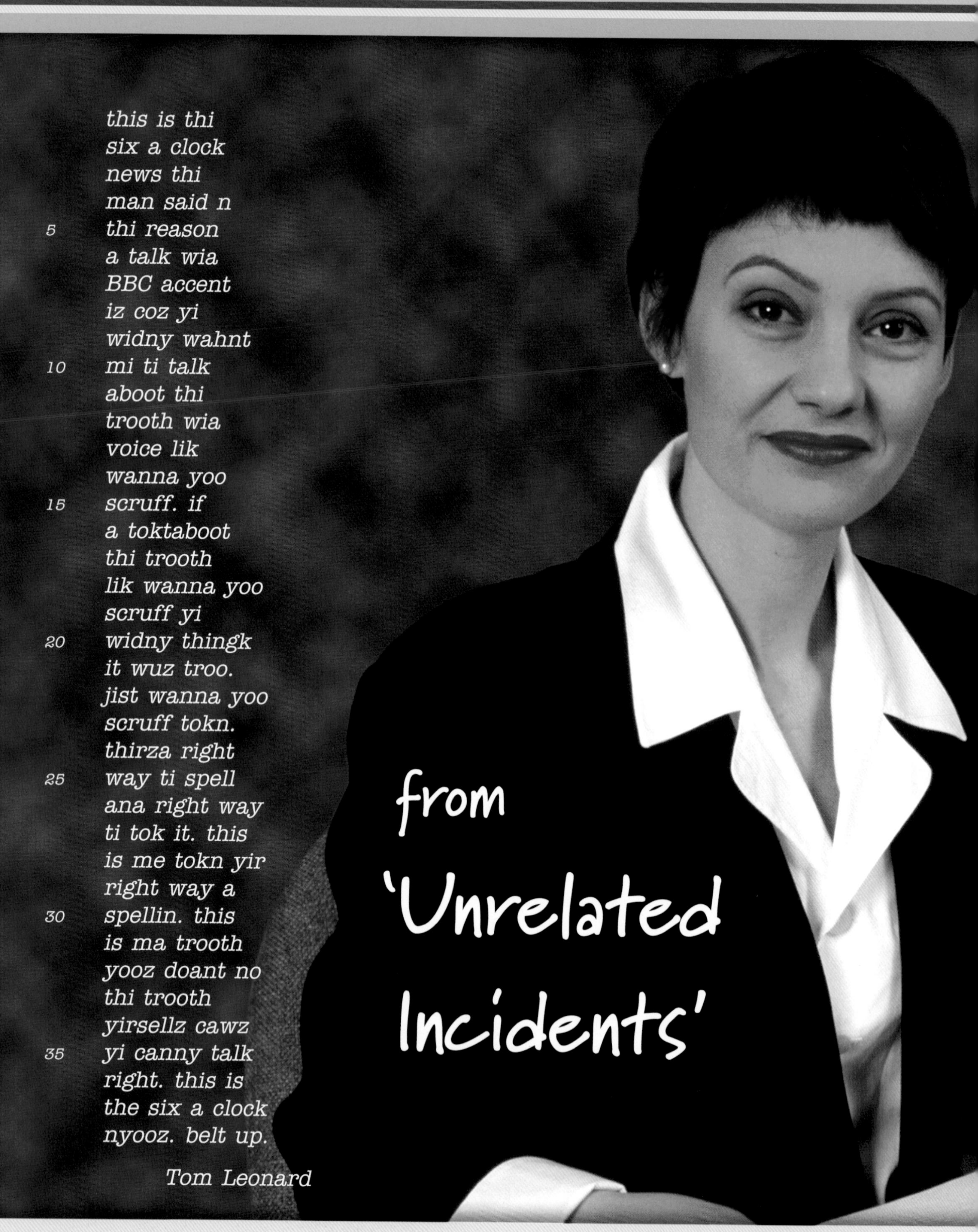

from 'Unrelated Incidents'

this is thi
six a clock
news thi
man said n
thi reason
a talk wia
BBC accent
iz coz yi
widny wahnt
mi ti talk
aboot thi
trooth wia
voice lik
wanna yoo
scruff. if
a toktaboot
thi trooth
lik wanna yoo
scruff yi
widny thingk
it wuz troo.
jist wanna yoo
scruff tokn.
thirza right
way ti spell
ana right way
ti tok it. this
is me tokn yir
right way a
spellin. this
is ma trooth
yooz doant no
thi trooth
yirsellz cawz
yi canny talk
right. this is
the six a clock
nyooz. belt up.

Tom Leonard

Exploring the poem

A newsreader with a broad Glaswegian accent reads the news. But it isn't the news as we know it. What's going on?

Think of the news broadcasts you have seen. Write about the expectations you have of the people that present the news. Is the woman in the photograph typical? Think about a typical newsreader's:

- dress
- behaviour
- way of speaking.

What might be the reaction of viewers if these expectations are not met? For example, would the *News At Ten* be the same if the main newscaster wore a T-shirt?

Ideas

Tom Leonard seems to be saying that many people are strongly prejudiced against certain regional accents. The newsreader in his poem is one of these people.

a. Write about the way the newsreader expresses his contempt for certain accents. Think about:
- the insult the newsreader repeats
- his closing insult
- why the newsreader believes regional viewers 'don't know the truth'.

b. What makes the newsreader's contempt for regional accents strange?

Language

The poem is written in a phonetic version of a Glaswegian accent with some of the punctuation missing.

a. Why do you think Tom Leonard has chosen to do this?
b. Write the poem in Standard English as a piece of prose.
c. Explain how your Standard English version may make the audience react differently from the way it would react to Tom Leonard's.
d. Why does Tom Leonard use repetition – and some very short sentences?

Structure

a. What is unusual about the presentation of the poem?
b. What reasons might Tom Leonard have had for presenting the poem in this way?

FINAL TASK: YOUR REACTIONS

Write a fuller piece, exploring why you think Tom Leonard wrote this poem. Take into account the discussions and work you have done.

Consider, as part of your response, the fact that the poem was written over 25 years ago. Do you thin that things have changed since that time? Does the poem still have important things to say to us toda

Half-Caste

Excuse me
standing on one leg
I'm half-caste

Explain yuself
5 *wha yu mean*
when yu say half-caste
yu mean when picasso
mix red an green
is a half-caste canvas/
10 *explain yuself*
wha yu mean
when yu say half-caste
yu mean when light an shadow
mix in de sky
15 *is a half-caste weather/*
well in dat case
england weather
nearly always half-caste
in fact some o dem cloud
20 *half-caste till dem overcast*
so spiteful dem dont want de sun pass
ah rass/
explain yuself
wha yu mean
25 *when yu say half-caste*
yu mean tchaikovsky
sit down at dah piano
an mix a black key
wid a white key
30 *is a half-caste symphony/*

Explain yuself
wha yu mean
Ah listening to yu wid de keen
half of mih ear
35 *Ah lookin at yu wid de keen*
half of mih eye
and when I'm introduced to yu
I'm sure you'll understand
why I offer yu half-a-hand
40 *an when I sleep at night*
I close half-a-eye
consequently when I dream
I dream half-a-dream
an when moon begin to glow
45 *I half-caste human being*
cast half-a-shadow
but yu must come back tomorrow
wid de whole of yu eye
an de whole of yu ear
50 *an de whole of yu mind*

an I will tell yu
de other half
of my story

John Agard

'Half-Caste'

Beginnings can set the tone for a piece of writing. Re-read these three lines from the start of the poem.

'Excuse me
Standing on one leg
I'm half-caste'

'Half-Caste' is not an expression used much nowadays. In the past, it was used to refer to people who had been born of mixed marriages. Why do you think the phrase is now seen as racist?

Look again at the first line of the poem.

a. When do people normally use this phrase?
b. Why is it ridiculous for the poet to use the phrase?
c. What do you think the poet is really saying to people who call him a half-caste?

Now look again at the second line.

d. Why is the poet doing this?
e. How does this action support his feelings?

Prejudices

People are often labelled as one thing or another because of the way they look or speak or act. The poet believes he is being labelled as half a person because he is neither 'black' nor 'white'.

a. Discuss with a partner some of the prejudices that you have come across in your everyday life. These do not need to be colour related, but could be related to speech, behaviour, skills – or lack of them – or many things.
b. Explain how these prejudices prevent people from seeing the 'whole' person.
c. Picasso was the Twentieth Century's most famous painter. How is he being used to support the poet's message? Why do you think the poet chose to use Picasso in particular?

Explain yuself
wha yu mean
when yu say half-caste
yu mean when picasso
mix red an green
is a half-caste canvas/

This painting by Pablo Picasso shows a vibrant mix of colour.

Reactions

Labels stop people from having to think. It is easier to pigeon-hole someone than to understand them.

a. How do you think people who have been labelled generally react to their treatment?

b. What do you think is the best way for them to challenge the labels and prejudices of others?

Extended practice

Write clear answers to the questions below.
Each deals with a different aspect of the poem.

Half a person?

a. List some of the imaginary actions the poet performs as half a person.
b. What effects might the poet want to create by describing himself in this way?
c. How does the emphasis change towards the end of the poem?

The poet's voice

a. What demanding phrase does John Agard repeat four times?
b. What tone of voice do you imagine him using at these points?
c. How do you think he feels when he makes the demands:
Aggressive? Mocking? Hurt? Amused? Insulted?

A celebration of mixtures

a. Which artist apart from Picasso does John Agard use to celebrate mixtures?
b. What else does he describe as mixed?
c. Why do you think he chose this other example of a mixture?

Types of language

Agard combines two different kinds of English in his poem.
a. Find examples of both his own dialect and Standard English.
b. Explain why he has used this method of presenting his ideas.

FINAL TASK: CONFRONTING PREJUDICE

At the beginning of this unit you wrote about some of the different ways people can confront ignorance and prejudice. Explain the different ways that John Agard stands up to being labelled a half-caste. Write about his use of:

- humour
- aggression and anger
- common sense
- language.

Love After Love

The time will come
When, with elation,
You will greet yourself arriving
At your own door, in your own mirror,
5 *And each will smile the other's welcome,*

And say sit here. Eat.
You will love again the stranger who was your self.
Give wine. Give bread. Give back your heart
To itself, to the stranger who has loved you

10 *All your life, whom you ignored*
For another, who knows you by heart.
Take down the love-letters from the bookshelf

The photographs, the desperate notes,
Peel your own images from the mirror.
15 *Sit. Feast on your life.*

Derek Walcott

Exploring the Poem

Sometimes it can be helpful to draw an image mentally (perhaps even draw a real one) to help you picture a poem. In this case, an illustration has been drawn for you.

a. Discuss with a partner – does the image make you think of:
- a new beginning
- a welcome
- something else altogether?

First impressions – words

In poems, the words themselves have to act as images. So what impressions do we get from them?

First of all consider how we say that people are 'in love with themselves'. What do we mean by this?

'Love After Love' is a poem about a man who has learned to love himself, either again or for the first time, and is recommending it to other people. How is his love for himself different from what we normally understand by 'self-love'?

Close study

The narrator's experience

a. How could the things the narrator tells us to 'take down' cause unhappiness?
b. What do you think he means by the phrase, *'Peel your own images from the mirror'*?
c. What experience do you think the narrator may have been through?

The extended metaphor of hospitality

a. How does the metaphor develop throughout the poem?
b. Why is this metaphor useful in expressing the poet's ideas?

Poetic techniques

How has the poet used:
- repetition
- enjambment
- sentences and lines of different length
- imperative verbs?

The advice

a. What advice is being given to readers of the poem?
b. Do most people take this advice or ignore it in their daily lives?

FINAL TASK: THE POEM'S MESSAGES

Imagine the poem 'Love After Love' is given by a large company to all its new employees. What messages do you think the management want their workers to take from the poem?

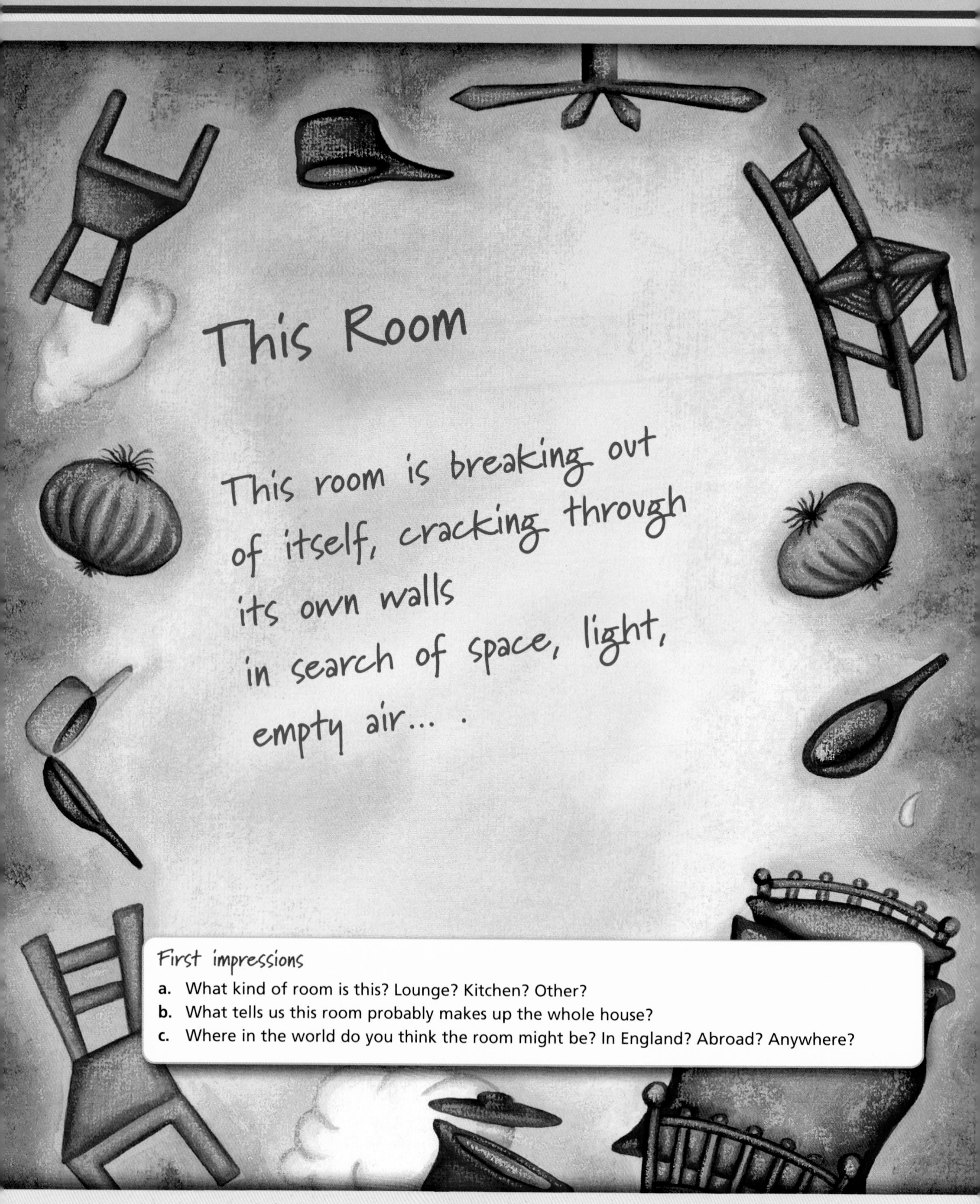

This Room

This room is breaking out
of itself, cracking through
its own walls
in search of space, light,
empty air... .

First impressions

a. What kind of room is this? Lounge? Kitchen? Other?
b. What tells us this room probably makes up the whole house?
c. Where in the world do you think the room might be? In England? Abroad? Anywhere?

The poet's craft

First lines

The words in the illustration are the first lines from the poem 'This Room'.

a. How do they change the way you view the picture?
b. Why do you think the room is 'breaking out of itself'?
c. What do the lines tell you about the writer's feelings?
d. What do you think the room and the writer are looking for?

Thinking like the poet

Think of a room you know very well, and choose three or four different pieces of furniture in it. Turn these into metaphors for unhappiness or frustration by writing about them as if they had feelings. You could try to describe:

- why each piece of furniture might be unhappy
- how the frustration is bottled up, day after day.

You could try:

> - a wardrobe - every day the same - a brief glimpse of daylight and then plunged back into darkness
> - a bookshelf - weighed down with closely packed books and photographs.

When you have done this, write about what each piece of furniture might do as an individual act of rebellion.

You could write:

> The wardrobe shook on its rickety base. The hangers inside rattled with pleasure as the doors began to splinter.

Now turn the page and read the poem 'This Room' before completing the task below.

Personification

Your description of a room has been based on personification. When poets use personification they write as if objects with no life of their own had human thoughts and feelings.

a. How has the poet used personification in the first lines of 'This Room'?
b. How do the line divisions support the message?

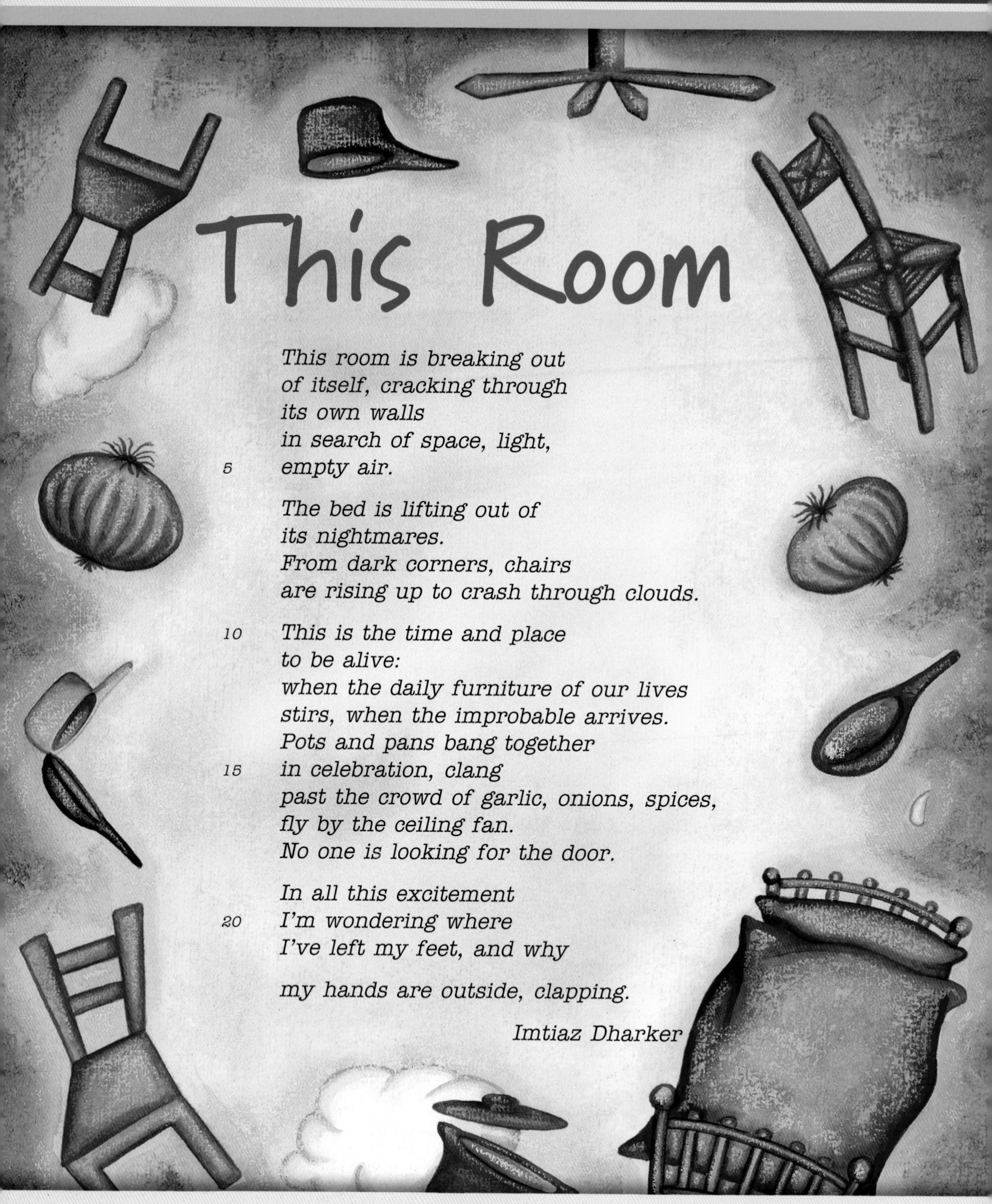

This Room

This room is breaking out
of itself, cracking through
its own walls
in search of space, light,
5 *empty air.*

The bed is lifting out of
its nightmares.
From dark corners, chairs
are rising up to crash through clouds.

10 *This is the time and place*
to be alive:
when the daily furniture of our lives
stirs, when the improbable arrives.
Pots and pans bang together
15 *in celebration, clang*
past the crowd of garlic, onions, spices,
fly by the ceiling fan.
No one is looking for the door.

In all this excitement
20 *I'm wondering where*
I've left my feet, and why

my hands are outside, clapping.

Imtiaz Dharker

Exploring the poem

Writing creatively yourself is a very good way into a poem, but let's look in more detail about how the actual text has been crafted.

Looking back

Discuss these questions with a partner:

a. Has your view of the room changed since you first saw the illustration?
b. How does the rest of the poem fit in with the first stanza?
c. Which parts of the poem remind you most of your own description of a room?
d. How do the personified objects in the poem express a feeling about being enclosed and in place?

Looking closely

The objects in the room seem to be escaping. Make brief notes for these questions:

a. What objects exactly are leaving the room?
b. Which verbs describe how they are leaving?
c. Describe the feeling that these verbs create.
d. What are the objects in the second stanza escaping from?
e. What do the pots and pans do as they escape?

Sound adds to the atmosphere

a. Find five words that draw attention to sound.
b. Why do you think onomatopoeia is such an important feature of this poem?

The focus of the poem changes in the last four lines

a. How does the focus change in these lines?
b. Describe the writer's emotions at the end of the poem.
c. How is the writer linked to her room?

The structure supports the message

a. Why are the verses divided in this way?
b. What effect is created by enjambment?

FINAL TASK: THE POEM'S MESSAGE

'This Room' could be interpreted as a poem about having the courage to change, or a poem about what is possible in life.

a. Why does it take courage to change the order and place of things?

b. What is the poet saying about the way we live?

c. Is her message convincing? Why/why not?

Not my Business

They picked Akanni up one morning
Beat him soft like clay
And stuffed him down the belly
Of a waiting jeep.
5 What business of mine is it
So long they don't take the yam
From my savouring mouth?

They came one night
Booted the whole house awake
10 And dragged Danladi out,
Then off to a lengthy absence.
What business of mine is it
So long they don't take the yam
From my savouring mouth?

15 Chinwe went to work one day
Only to find her job was gone:
No query, no warning, no probe –
Just one neat sack for a stainless record.
What business of mine is it
20 So long they don't take the yam
From my savouring mouth?

And then one evening
As I sat down to eat my yam
A knock on the door froze my hungry hand.
25 The jeep was waiting on my bewildered lawn
Waiting, waiting in its usual silence.

Niyi Osundare

Exploring the poem

From the first stanza

- Which two verbs emphasise the brutality of the authorities?
- How does the simile suggest that Akanni is badly beaten?
- How is the jeep personified?
- Explain the sinister effect of this personification.

From the second stanza

- Which two verbs stress the aggression of the police?
- What is the official sounding phrase in this stanza?
- Why do you think the poet might have chosen it?

From the third stanza

- How is Chinwe's experience different from Akanni's and Danladi's?
- How is her experience similar?
- Why is Chinwe's sacking so unfair?
- Which word is repeated three times in one line?
- How does this repetition emphasise the attitude of the authorities?

Looking at all three stanzas

- What is the narrator's main priority in life?
- Why is this priority repeated at the end of each stanza?
- What are the advantages and disadvantages of the narrator's approach?
- How are the authorities identified?
- What is the effect of giving names to the victims and not to the authorities?

The final stanza

- How is the first line of the stanza similar to the other first lines?
- What does this suggest about the power of the authorities?
- What is the narrator doing as he is about to be arrested?
- Explain the irony in what the narrator is doing.
- Why is the layout different from the other stanzas?
- How do the linguistic techniques help to make the stanza memorable?

FINAL TASK: THE WHOLE POEM

This is a poem with a very clear message.

a. Explain what the message is for you.

b. Is the message important for people who do not live in dictatorships?

Putting it all together

Students often have good ideas about poems but find it difficult to organise them in an exam. Some find they don't have enough time, while others find that although they can write at length they are not focusing on the task. It can also sometimes seem difficult to make meaningful comparisons between poems.

Assessment Objective

You need to show that you can *select material appropriate to your purpose, collate material from different sources, and make cross-references.*

Meeting this assessment objective in the time allowed can be a real challenge. The following example takes you through the process step-by-step.

EXEMPLAR TASK

Compare the way that authority is presented in 'Not my Business' and two other poems.

Stage 1 – Making sense of the task

You need to look for key words that tell you quickly what the task is about. In the exemplar task the key word is 'authority'. First, jot down other poems that deal with 'authority'. For example 'What Were They Like?'.

Stage 2 – Planning a response

Note down how 'Not my Business' addresses authority:
- Authority nameless/faceless.
- Authority vicious.
- Graphic descriptions of violence of authority.
- Actual victims of authority.
- Narrator confronts authority too late.

Now make notes on your second poem (in this case, 'What Were They Like?'):
- Authority formal/awkward.
- Army (authority) slaughter Vietnamese.
- Destructive power of authority clearly presented.
- Victims of authority entirely innocent.
- Narrator undermines authority.

Finally, choose a third poem that explores authority. Note down the points it raises.

EXAMINER'S TIP

Focus on the key word or words as you plan: this will ensure you are sticking to the relevant material.

A general structure

You can apply the following structure to your response whatever task you choose in the exam:

- A brief introduction.
- A discussion of poem 1.
- A comparison of poem 2 with poem 1.
- A comparison of poem 3 with poems 1 and 2 (if you are asked to write about more than two poems).
- A brief conclusion.

There will be more about making comparisons later on. The remaining stages of this guide will show you how to use the general structure to answer the exemplar question.

Stage 3 – Writing the introduction

Don't take up too much time on your introduction. It needs to be brief but clear. A good introduction will focus your own ideas on the task and show the examiner that you know where your response is going.

Example introduction 1

The three poems I am going to write about are 'Not my Business', 'What Were They Like?' and 'Two Scavengers in a Truck'. All these poems are about authority. In each of the poems, authority is an important issue. Authority is important because we all have to live in society and people with power should not be allowed to get away with whatever they want.

Example introduction 2

I am going to write about three poems. They are 'Not my Business', 'What Were They Like?' and 'Two Scavengers in a Truck'. I enjoyed reading each of these poems because they are about subjects I am interested in. The first poem is set in Africa and the other two are about America. I will spend an equal amount of time writing about each poem.

Example introduction 3

'Not my Business', 'What Were They Like?' and 'Two Scavengers in a Truck' all portray the exercise of authority. 'Not my Business' focuses on the way that individuals tend to ignore the misuse of power until it directly affects them. 'What Were They Like?' raises issues about the violence of authority and the way it can cause people to behave inhumanely. 'Two Scavengers in a Truck' explores the way in which social authority functions on a day-to-day level.

What are the strengths and/or weaknesses of these three introductions?

Stage 4 – Writing about the first poem

EXAMINER'S TIP

Speed is of the essence. In the exam, you'll have no more than about fifteen minutes for each poem. You won't have time to sift through the poems finding support for your points. Make use of the fact that you have been given the poems in advance and revise them well.

The notes on page 122 can be developed into a full response to the first poem. If your plan is a good one you'll be able to develop each separate point with quotations and evidence in support. The points from the plan are highlighted in the exemplar paragraph.

Exemplar paragraph

In 'Not my Business' **authority is presented as nameless and faceless**. The authorities are only ever called 'they' and it is unclear throughout the poem who exactly is being referred to. This lack of personality makes the authorities appear sinister. 'They' are a group of people without identity and this suggests they cannot be confronted. The **viciousness of the authorities** is emphasised by the verbs used to describe their actions. When they confront people they 'beat' them and 'boot' houses awake in the dead of night. The vicious nature of authority is also presented as something not necessarily involving physical aggression. One of the characters, Chinwe, has her livelihood taken away without reason or warning.

On the whole, however, the **violence of authority is presented in a graphic way**. The uncomplicated simile 'soft like clay' is a simple and chilling way of describing one victim's condition after a beating. The victim is 'stuffed ... down the belly of a waiting jeep'. The personification of the vehicle creates the impression of a hungry, ruthless beast. It is noticeable that while authority itself is faceless, **the victims are real people**. They are given names, 'Akanni', 'Danladi' and 'Chinwe' that force the reader to identify with them and the pain they confront. They are portrayed as normal humans doing normal things, like sleeping at home, going to work and eating their favourite foods.

Unfortunately, **the narrator confronts authority too late**. The title of the poem, 'Not my Business', suggests that he is prepared to turn a blind eye to the misuse of power unless it affects him. He is happy to enjoy his yam in peace and ignore the sufferings of others. His eventual fate indicates that this approach is not a wise one.

Points to remember

- Stay focused on the task.
- Deal with the points from your plan in a systematic way.
- Support your points with short quotations and explanations.
- Use technical terms like 'simile' and 'personification' but always explain their effects.
- Write in the present tense, using words like 'suggests' and 'indicates' to show poetry can be interpreted in different ways.

Stage 5 – Comparing a second poem with the first one

The key to making good comparisons lies in asking similar questions of different poems. In Stage 2 we looked at a basic plan that noted down the way 'Not my Business' and 'What Were They Like?' presented authority. Now we can see how the five points of each plan can be rewritten as questions that are the same for each poem.

EXAMINER'S TIP

Use these questions *before* the exam for revision purposes. Don't waste valuable time thinking them up on the actual day!

1. How do people in authority appear?
2. What does authority do?
3. How is the power of authority presented?
4. Who are the victims of authority?
5. How does the narrator relate to authority?

A series of questions will force you into making comparisons. For example, look at the answers to the first two questions here.

Comparison 1: How do people in authority appear?

In contrast with authority in 'Not my Business', authority in 'What Were They Like?' has a human voice. The speaker, possibly an army or a government spokesperson, sounds awkward and formal. He calls the questioner, 'Sir' and uses the passive voice in phrases like: 'It is not remembered'. It is almost as if he is trying to sidestep the questions and shift the blame to someone else. The authorities in Niyi Osundare's poem are hidden and so have no need to answer to anyone.

Comparison 2: What does authority do?

While the authorities in 'Not my Business' attack civilians of their own country, those in Denise Levertov's poem attack foreigners. Their aim seems to be to obliterate the Vietnamese. 'The children were killed' and 'bones were charred' in the rush to wipe out not only the people but also all signs of their culture. The goal of the Americans is presented as total victory rather than the ongoing control desired by the authorities in 'Not my Business'.

Now use the *three remaining questions* and the notes from Stage 2 to write three more comparisons between 'Not my Business' and 'What Were They Like?' similar to the two you've just read.

Stage 6 – Comparing a third poem with two others

Look back at the notes you made for a third poem to compare with 'Not my Business' and 'What Were They Like?'. Have you asked questions that are similar to those asked of the two others? If you haven't, make the notes again so that the points of comparison are clearer.

Here are exemplar notes for 'Two Scavengers in a Truck':

- Authority confident/attractive.
- Authority creates inferiority.
- Divisive power of authority emphasised.
- Ordinary people undermined.
- Narrator contemptuous of authority.

Comparing the three poems

> Authority in 'Two Scavengers in a Truck' is presented very differently from the other two poems. Niyi Osundare and Denise Levertov see authority as an openly aggressive force in which the destruction is plain to see. Lawrence Ferlinghetti, however, portrays his 'two beautiful people' as attractive and confident, the kinds of people that others want to be. Their authority lies in their expensive clothes and their perfect grooming. The man is wearing a 'linen suit' whilst the woman's hair is 'so casually coiffed'. They see no reason to hide their authority or to feel guilty about it.

EXAMINER'S TIP

Effective comparisons are relevant and brief. The writer of this passage compares the appearance of authority in the three poems and then quickly moves on to write about 'Two Scavengers in a Truck', the main focus of the section.

Either continue the comparison of the first two poems with 'Two Scavengers in a Truck' or write a new comparison with a third poem of your choice.

Useful words and phrases for making comparisons include:

- *but, however, more, less*
- *in comparison with*
- *by contrast with*
- *one significant way in which the poems differ is*
- *an important similarity between the poems is.*

Stage 7 – Writing a conclusion

Like your introduction, your conclusion should be brief and relevant. Its purpose is to pull together the most important parts of your response and to summarise them efficiently for the reader. Your conclusion is not the place to start making new points.

Example conclusion 1

I have written about three poems, 'Not my Business', 'What Were They Like?' and 'Two Scavengers in a Truck'. I enjoyed reading all three poems because I like reading poetry that comes from different cultures from our own. I would recommend anyone to read these three poems.

Example conclusion 2

All three poems explore the exercise of authority. Niyi Osundare's poem focuses on the quiet yet brutal authority of a police state and the dangers of ignoring it. Denise Levertov portrays the authority of military power and highlights its indiscriminate destruction. Lawrence Ferlinghetti focuses on the way authority is exercised in a society that is supposed to offer opportunity for all. Although they deal with different situations, the poems are linked by their opposition to the misuse of power.

Example conclusion 3

'Two Scavengers in a Truck' is a searing criticism of American consumer society. Lawrence Ferlinghetti despises the couple in the Mercedes because they represent the false authority accessible to those with money and status. The man and woman, for all their beauty and wealth, are no use to anyone, not even themselves. They exist simply to create envy. This is not the case in the other two poems.

What are the strengths and/or weaknesses of each of these conclusions? Which one of them provides the most effective summary?

Revision advice

1. As you approach the exams you need to:
   - decide which of the poems you feel most confident with
   - select around eight that you are going to revise in depth.

2. Establish links between the poems and, in particular:
   - look for thematic links like isolation, exploitation, pride and anger
   - prepare to write about the poems in 'sets' of three or four.

3. Ensure that when you come to write about the poems you are able to show:
   - how and why they are structured in a particular way
   - how and why language is used.

4. Use the many resources available to you:
   - Approach your teacher as your main source of help.
   - Use this book with friends and people in your family.
   - Check the following websites for further information.
     www.bbc.co.uk/schools/gcsebitesize
     www.learn.co.uk
     www.schoolsnet.com
     www.homeworkhigh.co.uk

5. Choose some of the practice questions opposite and complete them in 45 minutes.

Practice questions

1. Compare 'Not my Business' with one or more poems that raise important issues. Write about the issues raised and the way language and structure are used to support each poet's ideas.

2. 'Love After Love' could be said to take an optimistic view of life. Select one or more poems that also have an optimistic message. Compare them with 'Love After Love', saying what the poets feel positive about and how they express their optimism.

3. Compare 'Search For My Tongue' with one or more poems that explore social exclusion. Write about:
   - different types of exclusion in each poem
   - the ways the poets express their ideas
   - what the poems tell us about cultures.

4. Compare 'Half-Caste' with one or more poems in which language is used skilfully to express ideas.

5. How do 'Two Scavengers in a Truck' and one or more poems convey ideas about cultural conflict? Write about:
   - different kinds of cultural conflict
   - ways in which language is used to emphasise conflict
   - the ways ideas about conflict are organised.

6. Compare the ways in which 'What Were They Like?' and one or more poems confront ignorance.

7. Compare 'Unrelated Incidents' with one or more poems in which the writers demonstrate strong emotion. What are the poets emotional about and how do they express the strength of their feeling?

8. Select one or more poems and compare them with 'Island Man'. How do the poets make use of language and structure to help them convey their thoughts and feelings?

Paper 2, Section B: Writing to inform, explain, describe

Unit 10: **A writing process**

In this unit, you will:

- revise the planning process for Section B responses
- practise the routines involved
- complete the writing process, including checking work for errors.

Planning

In Unit 5, a planning process was described, using four stages:

1. identifying purpose and audience, underlining or highlighting important elements in any title
2. producing a spidergram of ideas
3. developing a detailed plan:
    - putting your ideas into logical order
    - adding notes to each idea, to indicate the content of each section
4. adding a palette of discourse markers, words and phrases to support your writing.

The same planning system can be used for Section B questions in both Paper 1 and Paper 2.

TASK 1

Complete the planning process for the following title:

Describe the person you most respect.

In your response, you might wish to write about:

- how you got to know them
- their qualities
- how they have influenced you.

In the examination, planning should take approximately five minutes, leaving:

- 35 minutes for writing; only about two sides are required
- five minutes to check and improve the response.

Where does it fit?

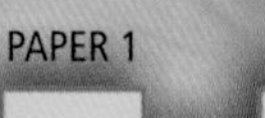

PAPER 1	PAPER 1	PAPER 2	PAPER 2
			✔
SECTION A	SECTION B	SECTION A	SECTION B

Writing

Your response will be judged on:
- ideas and structure
- paragraphing and punctuation
- sentences
- use of language
- spelling and presentation.

Having planned carefully, you can concentrate on the other important skills whilst writing.

Remember:
1. Stick closely to your plan: otherwise your planning time will be wasted and your writing is likely to lack direction.
2. Reread the title every half-page, to ensure you are still writing for the correct purpose and audience.

TASK 2

Write the response you have planned.

Aim to use appropriate and varied:
- length of sentence and paragraph
- vocabulary.

Checking

Checking and correcting your response improves your mark.
To locate errors:
- Read your work slowly, as if reading out loud.
- Concentrate on each word.
- Read what you have actually written, not what you believe to be on the page.

Improve what you have written, but do so neatly because you are also marked on presentation.

EXAMINER'S TIP

Mechanical paragraphs – which are the same length and not well connected – are one sign of 'D' Grade writing.

'C' Grade paragraphs are coherent.

TASK 3

Check your response.

KEY SUMMARY

The writing process can be used for Section B responses on both papers.

Spend:
- 5 minutes planning your response precisely
- 35 minutes writing imaginatively and with control
- 5 minutes checking your writing and correcting it where necessary.

Unit 11: **Writing to inform**

In this unit you will:

- review the types of information you may be asked to provide
- explore the key features of informative writing
- analyse informative extracts
- practise writing informative texts.

What is writing to inform?

- Its purpose is to share knowledge in a way that is interesting and useful.

Good writing to inform:

→ provides useful facts
→ includes the writer's opinions on the subject matter
→ is organised clearly into paragraphs.

High quality writing to inform:

→ adopts a style appropriate to purpose and audience
→ uses examples and anecdotes to maintain reader interest
→ conveys an overall impression of the writer's personality.

45 MINUTES

Where does it fit?

PAPER 1	PAPER 1	PAPER 2	PAPER 2
			✔
SECTION A	SECTION B	SECTION A	SECTION B

Exploring key features

Different types of information

You will usually be asked to give information about:

- places — *the area in which you live, your school, a favourite place of yours*
- people — *relatives, friends, people you admire*
- issues — *homework, the Internet, health*
- activities — *hobbies, visits, sporting events*
- plans — *for holidays, for improvements to your school, for next year.*

TASK 1

The following extracts are from informative assignments. Read each one and say whether it provides information about a place, person, issue, activity, plan or a mixture of these.

- If you wear the wrong clothes then you can quickly become an outsider.
- This year I'm not going to forget my alarm clock.
- She does things without wanting a reward – her help for the homeless is a prime example.
- The middle of the village is a bit of a mess.
- Abseiling appeals to me because it combines freedom and danger.
- I can discuss almost anything with him because I know he won't snap.
- Some people want the wasteground turned into a park. Others want a supermarket.
- Acting in plays gives me a feeling of achievement.
- Although it's cold it has a friendly atmosphere.
- Computers can be used as a means of escape.

Successful informative writing

Provides factual details	*Facts provide the substance of informative writing.*
Includes opinions	*Opinions add personality to the facts you provide.*
Is well organised	*Divide your subject up into logical parts, each with its own paragraph.*
Uses an appropriate style	*Consider why you are writing and who you are writing for. If your purpose and audience is personal, your style is likely to be informal.*
Uses examples and anecdotes	*They will help 'place' your information in the real world.*
Conveys an impression of the writer	*The choice and presentation of material should convey a sense of the person behind the facts.*

Source

The following letter was written by the actor Kenneth Williams to two friends in July 1969. Williams was famous for his performances in the *Carry On* series of films. In his letter, he mentions Brian Jones, a musician in the Rolling Stones, who had just died in mysterious circumstances. He also refers to the popular slapstick comedian, Benny Hill.

My dear Tom and Clive,

Quite an eventful few days … we went to Hyde Park. There was a vast crowd of people there because the Rolling Stones were playing in the open air, and it all turned into a sort of memorial service for Brian Jones, who as you know was found dead in his swimming pool. Apparently Mick Jagger got up and spoke of him very movingly and quoted the poem 'He is not dead He is not sleeping …' and everyone got quite emotional. I don't know what's the matter with this rotten typewriter but the spacing seems to be all over the place. Yes, well then we left the park and had some tea which was nice, and then in the evening we saw this marvellous film 'The Italian Job' with Noël Coward and Michael Caine. The ending is wickedly inconclusive and a bit of a cheat, but the rest of it is magnificently photographed and well cut. The only marred element is the casting of Benny Hill. You are asked to believe that he is Britain's cleverest computer expert, and of course you don't. He looks like a silly fat man, and no more suggests a mathematical intellect than fly in the air. The stunt stuff with the cars is terriffic. I mean terrific. It's this typewriter you see. Yes, well then we came out of there and walked in the heat of the evening to the Steak House for dinner. I had the wine etc., and then the Manager asked if I would have a brandy on the house! Well I thought – in for a penny, in for a pound – and so I had the brandy and then another and you can imajeen how I felt when I came out! Instead of going to the block I kept on walking. Went past the entrance. Would you believe reeled? and tottered along crying out 'Hallo dearie' to all and sundry.

Developing skills and techniques

TASK 2: AN INFORMAL STYLE

Kenneth Williams is writing about a set of personal experiences to people he knows well. His style is therefore very informal. The following exercises will focus your attention on different elements of his informal style.

a. Explain how the first sentence immediately shows informality.
b. Find two sentences where Kenneth Williams addresses his readers directly.
c. List three different words that are contractions.
d. Write down the word he deliberately misspells to show he was drunk.
e. Write down the direct speech Kenneth Williams uses to show he was drunk.
f. Kenneth Williams blames his typewriter twice. Explain two different responses he might be anticipating from his readers.

Rewrite the section from 'Yes, well then we came out of there ...' to the end of the passage using a formal style. Make sure you include all the information that Kenneth Williams provides.

g. Explain what you did to make this section formal.
h. Explain the effect of the changes.

TASK 3: ORGANISING THE INFORMATION

This letter would lose marks in an exam for not being clearly organised into three paragraphs.

a. List the three subjects that Kenneth Williams covers in his letter.
b. What two methods does he use instead of paragraphs to move from one subject to the next?

TASK 4: AN IMPRESSION OF THE WRITER

What impression do you form of Kenneth Williams from his writing? Support your opinions with evidence from the letter.

EXAMINER'S TIP

Convey an impression of your own personality when you are writing by providing more than just facts. Your personality will be reflected in your choice of informative detail, personal opinions, interesting examples and lively anecdotes.

Source text

The following article appeared in a travel magazine. It provides information about a hotel in West Virginia called *The Greenbrier.*

You wouldn't know it, as you pad across the luminous green acres, but you are leaving footprints on one of recent history's biggest geopolitical secrets. In a two-year construction project begun in 1959, the hillside beneath the hotel was chopped out to create space for a huge bunker designed to house Congress in the event of a nuclear attack. The entire, colossal subterranean compound was built in complete secrecy and with amazing speed and ingenuity. It seems impossible in retrospect. But people asked fewer awkward questions in the 1950s.

The Greenbrier Hotel

The Bunker might not be a secret any longer, but it could still be used. In an emergency, guests could be herded through the ballroom and the great steel door could swing shut behind them – and though the food wouldn't be quite what they had been promised, they could sit out almost any catastrophe.

Above ground, The Greenbrier is a sumptuous, upmarket retreat where it seems that nothing untoward could ever disturb the peace. It's not cheap, of course. But despite its time-honoured and faintly stuffy dress code (gentlemen are requested to wear jackets and ties in the dining room, if you please) it caters to every whim. The 1800 staff outnumber the guests: there's a specialist butter-waiter, and even the window cleaner sports a lapel badge – you just know he's the best goddamn window washer this side of the Rockies. The resort is sprinkled with goodies: its spa offers a 'Scotch Spray', which I imagine requires guests to wrap up warm and walk uphill through snow and hail. There are small pleasures wherever you turn, from the peach-flavoured iced tea decanted at the swimming pool to the 'skin-silkening' body gel in the showers. In an amazingly thoughtful touch, two ramps slant into the trout stream, so that disabled people can go fly-fishing. And it all comes wrapped in West Virginia's honey-drenched accent. At The Greenbrier this can be disconcerting: when the woman at the pool asked me how I was liking the 'green bra', I nearly answered that I liked it plenty but could have sworn it was white.

But it is, above all, a pinnacle of golf. In a lovely bowl of hills, criss-crossed by water, lie three fabulously groomed courses. This is golf the way it looks on TV: emerald expanses of grass in various shades; brilliant white sand in the bunkers; lordly trees; clear brown streams and blue lakes. Even the driving range is a cut above: you can slash your irons off the kind of polished lawn you might find in a cathedral precinct with 'Do Not Walk' signs all over it.

Developing skills (continued)

TASK 5: LOGICAL PARAGRAPHING

Unlike Kenneth Williams' letter, this article divides its sections clearly into paragraphs.

a. Write a summary statement for each paragraph, saying what it is about.
b. Write two more statements for other paragraphs that could have provided extra information.

When you have done this you will have an example of a six paragraph outline plan.

TASK 6: MIXING FACTUAL DETAIL WITH OPINIONS

The writer makes his article more interesting by combining facts with opinions.

a. Write down six facts provided by the writer.
b. List six opinions expressed in the writing.
c. Summarise the writer's overall opinion of the hotel.

TASK 7: A MORE FORMAL STYLE

The article is more formal than Kenneth Williams' letter.

a. With reference to audience, explain why this is.
b. Write down three sentences from Kenneth Williams' letter that would look out of place in this type of article. Explain why each one would be inappropriate.

TASK 8: USING EXAMPLES AND ANECDOTES

Read the third paragraph again and write down:

a. an example that clarifies the hotel's dress code
b. an example of the hotel's thoughtfulness
c. an anecdote that illustrates the West Virginian accent.

EXAMINER'S TIP

Using examples and anecdotes is one of the best ways of keeping a reader interested and engaged in your writing. Make the examples and anecdotes suitable for the sort of people who are your audience.

A candidate's response

Read the following question and answer.

Write a letter to a friend who is planning to visit a place you know well. Make your letter *informative*, useful and interesting to read.

The following paragraph was written in response to this task.

When you arrive in Kuala Lumpur you will probably fly into the new airport. After you have gone through customs you will either catch a bus or a taxi into the city centre. The middle of Kuala Lumpur is about 40 miles from the airport. It will take you roughly an hour to get there. There are a lot of hotels in the city centre. After you have booked into your hotel you will be able to do some sightseeing. There are a lot of museums and interesting buildings. The Petronas Towers are the tallest in the world and you can get an express lift to take you to the top. From the viewing gallery there are views of the city and the hills beyond.

The previous paragraph contains lots of factual information but it is not written in an interesting way.

In the next passage, the writer has conveyed similar information in a more successful way by using the techniques you have studied in this unit.

So you're going on holiday to KL! It's a brilliant place, a real mix of Malay, Chinese and Indian culture. There's so much going on that you won't want to go to bed at night. Now you're probably thinking, 'I hope she's not going to bore me writing some tedious travel guide.' Well I'm not. You'll find your own way, but here are a few suggestions about things you can see and do.

Your first adventure will be negotiating the airport. I don't like it, even if it is very modern and impressive. I went there when it was first built and got lost it was so big. Every time I tried to find our departure lounge I just ended up wandering into a different shop. Apparently the airport was designed so that people would be channelled into retail outlets to buy more goodies.

Anyway, if you manage to get through the airport, you'll need to get a taxi into the city centre, which should (I say should) take about an hour. Have you been to the Far East before? If you haven't, the traffic might come as a shock. Sometimes it gets gridlocked for hours on end and nothing moves except the meter on the taxi. If you're lucky, though, you'll end up in the middle of town in time to see some of the city before dark. There are so many things to do, like going up the Petronas Towers, visiting the National Museum, taking a trip on the elevated railway – or simply indulging yourself in a delicious local meal from a hawker stall.

TASK 9

Look back at the six main elements of successful informative writing. Explain how the second passage uses each of these features in turn.

TASK 10

a. Read the following sentences.

i. Or perhaps you feel, like many others, that getting on a bike is simply too dangerous.

ii. I helped someone I didn't like to mend his puncture and we've been friends ever since.

iii. I lost three kilos in my first month as a regular cyclist.

iv. Did you know that cycling's a brilliant way to meet new people?

v. Maybe you think that cycling sounds just too much like hard work.

vi. These are valid objections but I think the benefits of cycling outweigh the disadvantages.

vii. And then there's the social side of it.

viii. Cycling is actually no more risky than any other form of transport and, although it may be hard work at first, you'll soon start to enjoy the physical benefits.

b. Find one sentence each that:

- provides factual information
- demonstrates informality
- provides an anecdote.
- expresses an opinion
- uses an example

c. Now work out the correct order of the sentences and write them down as a complete paragraph.

TASK 11

The passage below was written in response to the following task.

Write an article for a student magazine that provides <u>information</u> about teenagers and the attractions of television.

> Many teenagers watch a lot of television. They watch a wide variety of programmes. Some of the programmes are educational and some of them are entertaining. Quite often, teenagers' parents complain that their kids are watching too much television. They think they should be doing homework instead. Really, though, I would say that most parents watch as much television as anyone else. Parents do not often realise that it is important for their kids to be able to discuss the most popular programmes when they get to school. If they have missed watching something everybody else has seen then they will be excluded.

Write your own response to the task:

- using factual details and opinions of your own
- organising your ideas into paragraphs
- adapting style more appropriately to purpose and audience
- using examples and anecdotes
- conveying your own personality more successfully.

Extended practice

Read the following task:

Write an informative article for older people entitled 'The Modern School'.

The following extract is part of an A Grade response:

Do you remember your school days? Many older people do with a strange mixture of horror and fondness. My grandfather is full of stories about pipe smoking teachers throwing board rubbers at snotty nosed children in classes of fifty and more. In those days, if the stories are to be believed, children were terrified of their teachers. The kids always seemed to have a good time in spite of it all and the fear of authority certainly didn't turn them into little angels.

Many older people know that schools are different now but they're not always certain of the nature of the changes. Probably the biggest difference is that most schools work on a system of mutual respect between teachers and pupils. The students are no longer treated as aggravating nuisances who need (by whatever means necessary) to be kept quiet. If they behave like adults then students can expect to be treated in an appropriate way. Although there are obviously times when discipline is needed, it is now more of a last resort than an everyday expectation.

TASK 12

Continue this piece of informative writing. You could include sections on:

- class sizes
- clubs and societies
- educational visits
- modern learning aids.
- activities in the classroom
- uniform
- homework

Remember to use:

- effective vocabulary
- a range of sentence construction
- appropriate paragraphing.

Specimen exam questions

1. Write a guide for a website giving essential **information** about your local area. Make your guide lively and interesting.

2. Write an **informative** article for newcomers on what it takes to be cool and accepted by Year 11 at your school.

3. Most of us know people we admire. Choose someone you know well and write about them in a way that will **inform** readers of their strengths.

4. Write a letter to a local newspaper **informing** them of an activity in which you are soon to take part. It could be:
   - a play
   - a sporting event
   - a school visit
   - any other event in which you are about to take part.

5. How would you most like to spend Christmas? **Inform** your reader about your preferences and **describe** your ideal Christmas.

6. Should learning to drive be part of the post-16 school curriculum? **Inform** your reader about the need for this and **explain** what advantages would follow.

KEY SUMMARY

- Make your information both interesting and useful.
- Combine factual detail with personal opinions.
- Organise your material into clear paragraphs.
- Show sensitivity to purpose and audience.
- Use examples and anecdotes to maintain reader interest.

Unit 12: **Writing to explain**

In this unit you will:

- examine the types of things you may be asked to explain
- explore approaches to different kinds of exam task
- study the ways in which content, language and structure can help an explanation
- assess explanatory articles from *CosmoGIRL!* and *She*.

What is writing to explain?

- Its purpose is to make a subject very clear to a reader.

Good writing to explain:

→ focuses on the subject being explained
→ has a well organised structure
→ goes into the required amount of detail
→ uses language to aid clarity.

High quality writing to explain also:

→ sequences material and uses organisational techniques that help the reader
→ maintains an appropriate style throughout
→ employs personal references, examples and anecdotes
→ uses a range of explanatory words and phrases.

45 MINUTES

Where does it fit?

PAPER 1	PAPER 1	PAPER 2	PAPER 2
			✔
SECTION A	SECTION B	SECTION A	SECTION B

Exploring key features

The things you may be asked to explain

You will most often be asked to explain *emotions*, *events*, *people*, *processes* and *beliefs*. Here are some examples of the kinds of questions you may be asked:

1. **Many people can remember doing things in their childhood that they enjoyed very much. Write about some of the things you can remember doing when you were younger and explain why they made you happy.**

   The *emotion* to be explained is happiness. The *events* that need to be explained are those that caused the happiness.

2. **Write about a time when you successfully confronted a difficult problem. Explain what was difficult about the problem and how you managed to overcome it.**

   The *process* to be explained is what you did gradually to overcome your problem.

TASK 1

Read the following candidate's response:

One event that really made me happy was on my eighth birthday when my mum took me to Megabowl with three friends from school, Joe, Peter and Scott. It was the first time I'd had a special trip; before then, it had always been sandwiches and crisps, and a few boring games.

What was the event and why did it make the writer happy?

Approaches to different exam tasks

Once you have identified whether the question requires you to write about emotions, events, people, processes, beliefs or a mixture of these, you have the basis for your response. So, for Question 1, you could write about three or four events from your childhood.

TASK 2

Now write the first paragraph for Question 2. Begin:

One difficult problem I overcame was ... .

A model text

Read the following article from *CosmoGIRL!*

six WORDS that rocked my world

'Your brother depends on you now'

Kelly Dower, 15, has looked after her brother Ryan since he was born, two years ago. Her mum suffered with septicaemia and experienced seizures during his birth, so Kelly and her sister, Sarah, now 13, had to give up their free time to look after him.

"When Mum had Ryan, I knew straightaway my life was going to change. She had three epileptic fits during labour and it was very scary. Mum stayed in hospital for weeks and even now she can't walk far and needs help bathing. My parents divorced when I was three, and Ryan's dad wasn't around, so I had to help or Ryan would have been taken into care. I was excited about getting so close to my brother, but nothing prepared me for what I had to go through. There was no time to see my friends. I washed Ryan, dressed him, cooked tea and changed nappies. I was so worried about cot death, I checked on him every 20 minutes.

It was exhausting, and just before last Christmas I broke down. I couldn't eat and was depressed, so I saw a counsellor and she taught me not to keep things bottled up. Now I'm more open I feel better, although sometimes I cry myself to sleep worrying about us being taken into care. A home help looks after Mum and Ryan while I'm at school, and I do my homework before she leaves. If I'm stressed I talk to my friend Rachel or the mentors at Cornwall Carers who organise trips for people like me.

I've grown up a lot since I became a carer, and people often think I'm 18 or 19. Sometimes my responsibility scares boys off, but the good ones are impressed. I've sort of got a boyfriend now, but we'll see how it goes. At the moment all my time is dedicated to my family."

Developing skills and techniques

Focus on the subject being explained

TASK 3: BREAKING EXPLANATIONS DOWN

Kelly provides explanations of emotions, events, people, processes and beliefs. For each of these areas, say what exactly Kelly has explained. The first one is done for you.

Emotions: Kelly explains the fear and excitement she feels when she finds out she is going to look after Ryan. Then she talks about the depression and exhaustion she went through before last Christmas. She also explains her dread of being taken into care.

TASK 4: A WELL-ORGANISED STRUCTURE

In what ways does the structure of Kelly's article make her experiences more clear?

EXAMINER'S TIP

Use paragraph divisions not only to sequence material, as Kelly has done, but also to explain the same material from different perspectives.

TASK 5: THE RIGHT AMOUNT OF DETAIL

Imagine that you are the magazine editor and you want a longer article from Kelly. Choose at least five areas from the existing article that it would be helpful to cover in more detail. In each case, say why the extra detail would help the explanation. An example is done for you.

- Kelly's friendship with Rachel. This would be helpful because a lot of Kelly's explanation is about how she copes with the difficult life she's been landed with. It would be interesting to read about specific situations in which Rachel has helped Kelly survive. It would make Kelly's explanation of the process of survival more clear.

TASK 6: USING LANGUAGE TO AID CLARITY

List five words Kelly has used to help explain the emotional side of her experiences.

The following fragment, "I washed Ryan, dressed him, cooked tea and changed nappies ..." comes near the end of the first paragraph of Kelly's article. What does putting four verbs into one sentence like this help to make clear about Kelly?

A model text

Read the following article from *She*.

"I STARVED MYSELF DOWN TO $6\frac{3}{4}$ STONE"

When Mohammed Caunhye, 26, suffered anorexia, few people challenged him about his weight loss.

I realised I had a problem about a year after I became obsessed with dieting, when I started bingeing and purging. My mum bought me some popcorn and I ate loads of it. I then panicked about the food inside me – the only thing to do was throw it up.

Things got worse from there. I'd eat five or six bars of chocolate a day, or packets of biscuits, but it didn't matter because I could be sick afterwards. I also overexercised and ran for miles every morning. By now I'd left college and had started work as a trainee accountant, but the bulimia made it hard to concentrate and jogging so much made my limbs hurt constantly. I'm sure if I was a woman my colleagues might have noticed my weight loss, but as it was nobody did.

Everything changed when I spent a weekend with my family. My sister noticed that I was bingeing and purging, and forced the truth out of me. She then sent off for leaflets on anorexia and bulimia from Eating Disorders Anonymous (EDA). When I read them, I knew I had a problem. I went to a doctor for help, but she just put me on vitamins and prescribed painkillers for the aches in my limbs. My sister persuaded me to go to a meeting. It was strange because I listened to other people talking, and thought, 'That's me.'

Then, out of the blue, a college friend, Ceridwen, got in touch. We met up and had a fun time out. By the end of the night I realised I hadn't thought about food at all. We started dating and that meant going out for meals. She didn't know about my eating disorder and I tried to eat normally when I was with her.

When I did tell Ceridwen, she was so understanding. I wanted to be well for her so I stopped the purging. We got engaged in March 2000 and married in April this year. Living with Ceridwen normalised my eating. Food shopping with someone else forced me to think about her needs, too.

I'm still wary about fat and calories but I don't deny myself food when I'm hungry now and I've only made myself sick twice in the past year. Best of all, Ceridwen is pregnant and I couldn't be happier.

Developing skills (continued)

TASK 7: SEQUENCING MATERIAL

In this article, Mohammed explains his experience as a process of illness leading to recovery.

a. For each paragraph, write one sentence in summary. Your six sentences will then show the process of his experience. The first sentence is done for you.

- Mohammed started bingeing and purging.

b. Now look at your six summary sentences. On the basis of these, write one or two more sentences that summarise what Mohammed has explained over the whole article. You could begin

- Mohammed is making it clear to the reader … .

TASK 8: USING PERSONAL REFERENCES

a. In his third paragraph, Mohammed mentions three things he did to deal with his illness. Write down these three strategies.

b. Look at the three strategies you have identified. What is Mohammed trying to explain – make clear – about his experience by mentioning them?

c. Mohammed explains how, from the beginning, his relationship with Ceridwen has helped him through his eating disorder. Write down five separate ways that Mohammed says his relationship with Ceridwen has helped.

d. Now write your own article explaining how someone has helped you through a difficult stage in your life. Make sure that, like Mohammed, you provide lots of specific detail about your difficulty in the first place. Also, like Mohammed, try to give precise examples of how your chosen person has helped.

You can use Mohammed's paragraph structure to help you. For example, you could begin with the phrase

I realised I had a problem … .

EXAMINER'S TIP

Make any personal references in your writing support your overall explanation. Mohammed's personal references, for example, all contribute to a general understanding of his experience of bulimia.

Developing skills

Using organisational techniques

Kelly and Mohammed made their experiences as clear as they could for readers they had not met. You must ask yourself how you can make your subject as clear as possible to a reader who does not know you.

A GCSE student, Sean, faced the following task:

Many people find pleasure in the everyday things of life rather than in big events. Write about some of the ordinary things that you do and explain why you enjoy them.

Sean immediately asked himself the following question: How can I make my enjoyment of ordinary things clear to the reader? He answered it like this: The best way to make it clear would be to choose four or five everyday activities and explain why I enjoy them so much.

Then Sean wrote down some of the ordinary things he did and noted why he enjoyed them:

- walking to school - *time to think/talk to friends*
- playing basketball - *keeping fit/competitive*
- cooking - *creative/relaxing/appreciated by others*
- talking to baby brother - *amusing/helpful to family*

TASK 9

Using exactly the same methods as Sean, respond to the following task:

Many people are irritated by everyday things. Write about some of the things that annoy you regularly and explain why you find them so aggravating.

Maintaining an appropriate style

You must maintain an appropriate style throughout your explanation. You should write in a way that is serious without being too formal. The following three sentences are all ways of beginning an answer to the task above:

Employing examples and anecdotes

Anecdotes and examples often make explanations more lively and clear. They can provide extra detail that is essential for the reader to gain a fuller understanding of what is being explained. The difference between anecdotes and examples can be seen in the sentences below.

- I enjoy cooking because it is creative.
- I enjoy cooking because it is creative. For example, you can mess around with herbs.
- I enjoy cooking because it is creative. For example, you can mess around with herbs; I once used basil instead of oregano in a bolognese sauce and it tasted great.

The third sentence is followed by an example and then an anecdote to support the original statement. In an exam you would usually present your examples and anecdotes in more detail.

TASK 11

Sean's notes on the opposite page refer to his enjoyment of cooking. The sentences above expand this original idea. Look at the notes you have made for the question on everyday things that irritate you. Select one of the ideas from your notes and expand it into a paragraph. Use examples and anecdotes as part of the expansion.

Using explanatory words and phrases

Use these **verbs** to explain what you think or feel about something:

- think/find/feel/believe/consider/suppose/guess.

Use these **modal verbs** when you want to explain that something is not certain:

- it may/could/might be.

Use these **phrases** to explain cause and effect:

- this is because/the reason for this/this happened when/as a result of this.

Use these **discourse markers** to introduce an anecdote or example:

- for example/for instance/one example is/once/on one occasion/one time/the other day.

TASK 12

Many of these words and phrases appear in the extract below. List them as they appear.

Something I find really irritating is bad TV. This might be because I don't watch much and my expectations are high. I do think, though, that standards are very poor. The other day, for example, I watched a documentary about war that ended up glamourising it. I guess the reason for this dumbing down may be to capture big audiences but it turns me off completely.

Extended practice

TASK 13

Read the following question:

Lots of people have favourite places – rooms, buildings, places outside. Write about some favourite places of your own and explain what makes them so special.

Remember the stages you need to go through before responding to the task:

- **What type of question is this?**
  This question asks you to explain the positive emotions created by places you like.
- **What question do you need to ask yourself?**
  You need to ask yourself how you can make it clear to the reader why your places are so special.
- **What is the best way to answer the question?**
  The best way to answer the question would be to list two or three places and then explain clearly why they are special in different ways. Use examples and anecdotes.
- **How do I impress the examiner?**
  Vary explanatory words and phrases.

Now prepare your answer to the question.

A candidate's response

The following extract is the first paragraph of an 'A' Grade answer:

> One of my favourite places is the bus shelter outside school. Most people would not think a bus shelter is very interesting, and would expect a favourite place to be somewhere exotic.
>
> I suppose the main reason I like it so much – at least in the winter – is because it is one of the few places anyone can keep dry and reasonably warm on a main road when you need to get off the school premises at lunchtime. If you still think a bus shelter is an odd place to choose, there are others who seem to share my odd choice. The other day, for instance, the shelter was packed full of people chatting and nobody got on to any of the buses that pulled up. You'll see now that it's not the décor or the architecture that makes the shelter a favourite place: it's the company, and the social diary. Yesterday, I met up there with three of my closest friends who I hadn't seen for three days. We solved the world's problems, swapped gossip and sorted out the weekend before getting back to Maths in Lesson 4. If you had to face Maths Lesson 4, you'd begin to see why the bus shelter is a favourite place.

Now write three more paragraphs yourself.

Specimen exam questions

1. In difficult situations we may have to rely on other people for help. Write about someone you would trust during an awkward time, making sure you **explain** why you think you could depend on him or her.

2. **Explain** some of the ways in which new technology has changed the way we live.

3. Write about a time when you stood up for yourself. **Explain** how and why you made your stand and how you feel about your actions.

4. Improvements can always be made to the areas in which we live. Write about alterations that could improve your area and **explain** how the changes would benefit you and people like you.

5. **Explain** what you think are the most important characteristics needed to be a good parent.

6. Write a letter to your local newspaper **explaining** why a new supermarket will be good or bad for the town and **describing** some of the likely effects of this development.

7. Write a letter to a friend **explaining** why you cannot join him/her on a camping holiday in France and **informing** him/her of how he/she can contact you from France.

KEY SUMMARY

- Focus on the subject you have been asked to explain.
- Structure and organise your writing so that it is clear.
- Provide the right amount of detail.
- Use personal references, anecdotes and examples.
- Employ explanatory words and phrases.

Unit 13: **Writing to describe**

In this unit you will:

- review the types of description you may be required to write
- assess the key elements of successful description
- read and analyse writing by the novelists Anita Desai and Iain Banks
- study successful GCSE descriptions.

What is writing to describe?

It is writing designed to create a vivid and compelling set of images in the mind of a reader, and to clearly convey the sense of a place, event, feeling or person.

Good writing to describe:

→ uses a range of imagery for different effects
→ appeals to the reader's senses
→ makes effective use of adjectives and adverbs.

High quality writing to describe also:

→ communicates the writer's attitude towards the thing being described
→ adapts and manipulates conventions
→ varies sentence and paragraph structure for effect
→ uses a variety of powerful verbs.

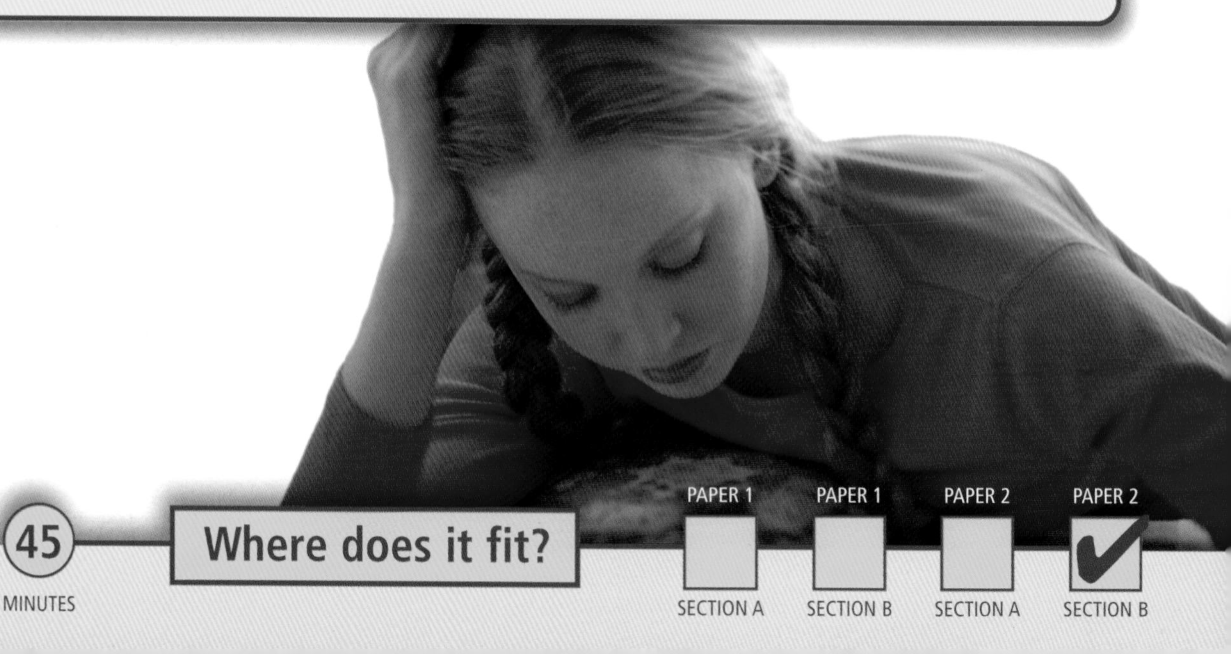

45 MINUTES

Where does it fit?

PAPER 1	PAPER 1	PAPER 2	PAPER 2
			✔
SECTION A	SECTION B	SECTION A	SECTION B

Exploring key features

Successful description

This passage uses some of the key features of successful descriptive writing.

abbreviated sentences for effect

metaphor

simile

adjectives build up a misty, desolate feeling

personification

adverbs create 'sleazy' impression

alliteration

strong, well-chosen verbs in the present tense

Late November. The centre of the city lies still as a tomb, grey in the cold earth. Silent buildings are gravestones to the living cemetery beneath. A chill wind blows the hair across my face. Dust and dirt swirl from the gutter and a tin can rattles down the pavement, its half consumed contents dribbling stickily behind. A cheeseburger carton limps unwillingly along before lodging beneath a bench. The smell of stale onions lingers from an abandoned hot dog stand. And beside me, in the wide shop door, a sign of life. A cardboard box shifts in the gloom and a dark shape shuffles. A cupped grey hand extends, yet I move away ashamed.

In the distance, the cars on the bypass busily hum.

TASK 1

Write two or three paragraphs describing the city centre at a busy time of the day. Use the passage and the techniques outlined to help you.

A model text

Read the following passage. It describes the scene in a small seaside town in August.

In that small town, clustered around and above the bay, every third house was a boarding house, while hotels were strung out along the promenade, stolidly gloomy all through the year except in summer when wet bathing suits hung out over every windowsill and sunburnt children raced screaming across the strip of melting asphalt and onto the shining sands, magnetised by the glittering, slithering metal of summer seas. Sand dunes, dune grass, shells, streams trickling across the beach, creating gulleys, valleys and estuaries in exquisite miniature and shades of purple, sienna and puce. Boat sails, surf boards, waves, foam, debris and light. Fish and chips, ice-cream cones, bouncy castles, spades, striped windbreakers. 'Where can I pee-pee? I have to pee-pee!' 'Spot, come away! Come away, Spot!' 'I've cut my foot! Ooh, look, boo-ooh!' And a hinterland of blackberry bushes, rabbit warrens, golf links, hedged meadows, whitewashed, slate-roofed farmhouses – and the motorway flowing all summer with a droning, steady stream of holidaymakers baking in their beetle-backed cars.

The White House Hotel alone appeared to take no part in this summer bacchanal. Summer and winter, spring and autumn, it remained the same: an immaculate whitewashed cottage built of Cornish stone, with a slate roof, red geraniums in green windowboxes, and wrought-iron gates shut to the road. Not exactly the kind of place you hoped to find when you came to the seaside – it was not far from the sea, true, but had no view of it. Instead, it looked out onto the long, low hills, their green downs speckled with the white fluffballs of grazing sheep, in their hollows the kind of woods that sheltered streams, bluebells, yellow flags and dragonflies. Pretty enough, but not providing that sense of being at the seaside which was what you came to this little town for, a hellish drive in August.

Anita Desai

Developing skills and techniques

TASK 2: USING LANGUAGE FOR EFFECT

Read the first sentence again and:

a. write down the verb that describes the action of the children

b. list three alternative verbs that might not have been so effective

c. write down the adverb and adjective that describe the hotels

d. write down two adjectives that describe the sea

e. explain the contrast that is set up between the hotels and the sea

f. explain the metaphor that is used to describe the sea and its effect on the sands.

TASK 3: EFFECTIVE SENTENCE AND PARAGRAPH STRUCTURE

a. Why do you think Anita Desai chose to make the first sentence so long?

b. Why do you think she chose to divide this description into two paragraphs?

c. Find the third and fourth sentences and explain what is unusual about them. Using the same technique as Anita Desai, write two sentences of your own to describe
   - a busy airport
   - a fast food restaurant.

TASK 4: MANIPULATING DIRECT SPEECH CONVENTIONS

a. How is the presentation of direct speech in this passage unconventional?
   - Who are the different speakers?
   - What are their feelings as they speak?
   - What mood is created as a whole by the direct speech?

b. Explain the reasons the writer may have had for presenting direct speech in this way.

EXAMINER'S TIP

If you choose to write a non-standard sentence or include some ungrammatical speech, make sure it is obviously deliberate. Anita Desai, for instance, deliberately presents speech in an unconventional way to create the impression of a babble of voices.

A model text

The following passage describes a run-down hotel at night.

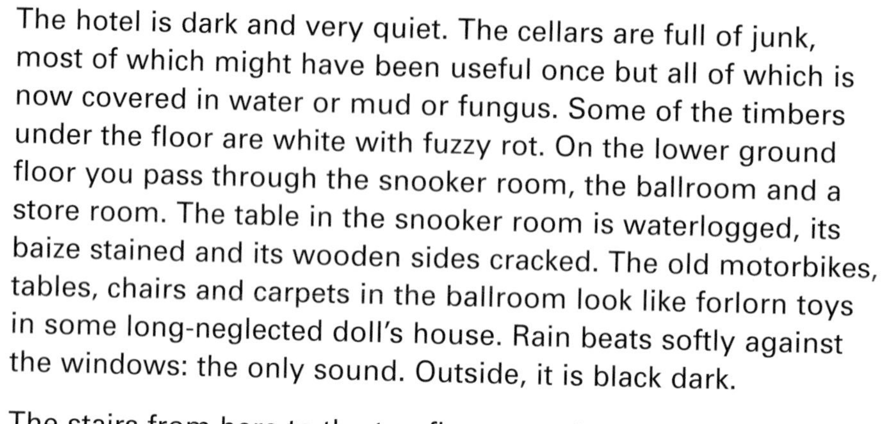

The hotel is dark and very quiet. The cellars are full of junk, most of which might have been useful once but all of which is now covered in water or mud or fungus. Some of the timbers under the floor are white with fuzzy rot. On the lower ground floor you pass through the snooker room, the ballroom and a store room. The table in the snooker room is waterlogged, its baize stained and its wooden sides cracked. The old motorbikes, tables, chairs and carpets in the ballroom look like forlorn toys in some long-neglected doll's house. Rain beats softly against the windows: the only sound. Outside, it is black dark.

The stairs from here to the top floor stretch upwards around the dilapidated grandeur of the stairwell. On the next floor up the reception area is dusty and bare, the bar smells of sour booze and stale cigarette smoke and the empty dining room is redolent of dampness and decay. The kitchen is cold and hollow and echoing. There is one old domestic stove, powered by bottled gas, and one sink. There's an apron hanging on a nail.

You take the apron and put it on.

The next two floors hold bedrooms. There is dampness here too, and in some of the rooms the ceiling has fallen in, the plaster and lath lying draped over the heavy, old-fashioned furniture like some clumsy travesty of a dust-sheet. The rain is hitting the windows harder now, and the wind is getting up, whistling through cracks in the panes and the window-frames.

The top floor feels a little less damp, a little more warm, though the wind and rain still sound loud outside and above.

At one end of the dark corridor, past the wedged-open fire door, a door lies ajar. The living room inside is lit by the remains of a log fire, collapsing now into ashes. A couple of logs lie on the hearth, drying, and the air smells of their pine scent and cigarette smoke. An old coal scuttle to the side of the fireplace holds a can of paraffin, almost full.

Iain Banks

Developing skills

EXAMINER'S TIP

Like Anita Desai and Iain Banks, show readers your attitudes rather than tell them what they are. Allow your feelings about a subject to emerge gradually through your description, in short phrases rather than explicit sentences.

TASK 5: THE WRITER'S ATTITUDE

Remember that good writing communicates attitudes without stating them directly. Both the passages you have just read communicate attitudes effectively.

Compare the writer's attitude towards the hotel with Anita Desai's attitude to the seaside.

TASK 6: USING IMAGERY

Write down the sentence that contains the simile in the first paragraph and underline the adjective that creates personification. Explain what the imagery suggests about the hotel.

TASK 7: AN APPEAL TO THE SENSES

Iain Banks makes good use of the sense of hearing in this passage.

a. What can the writer hear? Explain how what he hears demonstrates changing time and place.

The writer never tells us directly that someone is living in the hotel.

b. How does the writer show us there is life in the hotel?

c. Which two of the five senses does he use to do this?

TASK 8: MANIPULATING WORD ORDER CONVENTIONS

Read the following sentence:

'At one end of the dark corridor, past the wedged-open fire door, a door lies ajar.'

The subject of the sentence (what the sentence is about) usually comes at the beginning. In this sentence the subject is 'a door'.

Explain why the writer has chosen to place the subject near the end of the sentence.

Developing skills

Language, imagery and attitude

Read this description of a lighthouse.

The lighthouse goes up into the sky. I can see its spotlight and I can hear it moving around. I can also hear the waves. The waves are going in and out. Sometimes the waves splash over me. I look again at the lighthouse.

Now think back to why people write descriptions.

The purpose of writing a description is to create a vivid set of images in the mind of a reader.

The writer tells us what can be seen and heard but does not create any vivid or compelling images that allow the reader to visualise the scene.

This description is of the same lighthouse.

The lighthouse soars up into the cold night air. The low groan of its rotating spotlight struggles like the moan of a wounded animal through the crash and heave of surf below. Reluctantly the waves retreat, sucked back into the darkness, then angrily return, pounding the foot of the mighty stone structure. The spray showers over me and my mouth fills with the cold, salt taste of the sea. The lighthouse stands stern, a forbidding guardian of the shore.

This is much more successful. The writer has made it original and interesting and expressed an attitude. Look closely and you will see how language and imagery have been used to create an effective description.

TASK 9

a. Find and write down:
- one simile
- three examples of personification
- three examples of an appeal to the senses
- three adjectives
- one metaphor
- two examples of alliteration
- five powerful verbs
- two adverbs.

b. Now explain the attitude towards the scene communicated by the writer.

Sentence and paragraph conventions

As you have seen in earlier parts of this unit, this is one part of the English exam where it is possible, if you do so carefully, to adapt and manipulate grammatical conventions.

Look at these conventions:

- Do not begin a sentence with the word 'And'.
  The sun shone brightly.
  And the sun shone brightly.
- Use commas to divide words in lists, not conjunctions.
  It was cold, wet, damp and miserable.
  It was cold and wet and damp and miserable.
- The subject of a declarative sentence should come first.
  The smoke rose weakly from the dying embers.
  From the dying embers, the smoke rose weakly.
- Paragraphs should be longer than one sentence.
  See the example in Task 10.

TASK 10

Read this third description of the lighthouse.

> *And through the mist, the lighthouse soars up into the cold night air. The low groan of its rotating spotlight struggles like the moan of a wounded animal through the crash and heave and clatter of surf below. Reluctantly the waves retreat, sucked back into the darkness, then angrily return, pounding the foot of the mighty stone structure. The spray showers over me and my mouth fills with the cold, salt taste of the sea.*
>
> *A forbidding guardian of the shore, the lighthouse stands stern.*

a. Write down the sentences that have 'manipulated the conventions'.

b. Why is the one-sentence paragraph effective?

c. Describe a landmark you know well, manipulating conventions as in this example.

EXAMINER'S TIP

When you are writing, consider using the present tense for description – it might help you avoid too much storytelling.

Extended practice

Look at the following question:

Describe a walk through the woods. You could write about a real or imagined experience.

A candidate's response

The following response to this question is part of an A Grade answer:

Overhead, the gentle hand of the wind rustles the leaves. A lonely leaf drifts down to the dark greenness of the forest floor. A single shaft of yellow sunlight marks my way as I tread silently on along the path. Trees surround me, forcing their way out of the fertile earth, straining for the light above. Bushes and shrubs wrestle with each other in the lower shade. Ahead, an arm's length away, a squirrel darts from the undergrowth. It stops and turns and stares, rigid as a toy soldier. I stop for a moment too. The squirrel seems suddenly to lose its nerve and scampers off.

The wind is stronger now, surging noisily through the tops of the trees. The path slopes suddenly towards a gully and I trip and stumble on. A small stream sparkles, catching the sunlight, a dazzling necklace in the forest gloom. The stream sings across the pebbles as I reach its mossy edge. Kneeling down, I cup my hands and raise the clear, cold water to my mouth. I can taste the woody earth. An old footbridge spans the stream and I look down as I cross. Twigs and leaves and petals float along like miniature travellers to distant unknown lands.

And now, it is suddenly darker.

TASK 11

List examples of where the writer has:

- used imagery
- appealed to the reader's senses
- used effective adjectives and adverbs
- varied sentence and paragraph structure
- used powerful verbs.

TASK 12

Now complete the description of the woodland walk. Alternatively, write about a visit to a crowded shopping centre. You will gain marks by using the skills you have studied in this unit.

Specimen exam questions

1. Think of a place you know well. **Describe** it during and after a storm.

2. Write a **description** of your school during breaktime.

3. **Describe** one of the following so that it can be easily imagined by your reader:
   - A leisure centre.
   - The home of an elderly relative.
   - A school trip.

4. Write about somewhere interesting you have been on your holidays. Concentrate on **describing** one or two locations in detail.

5. **Describe** your bedroom as it usually is on a Sunday and **explain** how it gets into that state and what this says about you.

6. **Describe** the scene in a CD store on Saturday and **explain** what connections you see between different people and the CDs that they buy.

KEY SUMMARY

- Create vivid images in the mind of the reader.
- Use imagery and appeal to the senses.
- Make effective use of adjectives, adverbs and verbs.
- Vary your sentence and paragraph structures.
- Adapt and manipulate conventions for effect.
- Communicate an attitude towards what you are describing.

Final preparation for the examination

This book has taken you through the skills needed for the examination, and you have dealt with the sorts of materials you are likely to encounter. The final touches of preparation will be in your own hands; but what, exactly, should be done to prepare properly?

1. Revise

Revision is the key to success.

Paper 1, Section A
Read non-fiction and media texts and test yourself against the Assessment Objectives.

Consider:

- facts and opinions, and how they are used
- how information is presented
- how arguments are constructed, their implications and inconsistencies
- how linguistic, structural and presentational devices are used, and how language varies and changes
- comparisons between texts.

Paper 1, Section B
You will be writing to argue, persuade or advise.
Practise producing responses quickly, completing the planning and writing process.

Paper 2, Section A
Decide which poems you would most like to write about, and prepare them thoroughly in groups of three or four.

Revise:

- exactly what they are saying
- how the poets have used linguistic and structural devices to support their ideas.

Have a working knowledge of the other poems, just in case the title requires you to write about them.

Practise producing responses in just 45 minutes.

Paper 2, Section B
You will be writing to inform, explain or describe.

Follow the same routine as for Paper 1, Section B: practise planning and producing a response in just 45 minutes.

2. The day of the examination

For the day of the examination, make sure you get everything right.

Know:
- the date of each examination, and when you need your *Anthology*
- when each examination begins, and where it is taking place.

Arrive in plenty of time and with the correct equipment.

Do not panic.
- Read the paper quickly but thoroughly.
- Ensure you know exactly what each question is demanding – if necessary, underline the most important words in each question, to focus your attention.
- Think clearly – if, for example, you want to tackle a question on Paper 1, Section B, which demands a mixture of argument, persuasion and advice, you can cope; in this instance, you will blend your knowledge from the three different units in this book.
- Keep your eye on the clock – you should have practised completing responses in the required time; but it is no good practising if you go to pieces on the Big Day!
- Plan your responses for Section B.
- Try to check all your writing, and correct it when necessary.

Remember that the examiner wants to reward your efforts.

Your task is to present work that allows the examiner to award top marks.

General Certificate of Secondary Education
Practice Paper

ENGLISH A
Paper 1

Time allowed: 1 hour 45 minutes

Instructions
- Use blue or black ink.
- Answer **all** the questions in **Section A** and **one** question from **Section B**.
- Spend about 1 hour on Section A and the rest of your time on Section B.
- Cross through any rough work you do not want to be marked.
- You must not use a dictionary in this examination.

Information
- The maximum mark for this paper is 54.
- Mark allocations are shown in brackets.
- You are reminded of the need for good English and clear presentation in your answers.
- All questions should be answered in continuous prose.

SECTION A: READING

Read Item 1, the newspaper article 'Iceberg in a bottle set to wash over UK' and Item 2, the article from a newspaper website 'Slowly but surely, Iceland is losing its ice – Global warming is prime suspect in meltdown'.

Answer **all** the questions in this section.
Spend about **60 minutes** on this section.

Read Item 1, the newspaper article 'Iceberg in a bottle set to wash over UK'.

Examining it as a media text, answer the following questions:

1. a. What is the purpose of the article and what is the likely audience?
   b. How effective are the layout and presentation?
   c. How is the article structured?

(8 marks)

Read Item 2, the article from a newspaper website 'Slowly but surely, Iceland is losing its ice – Global warming is prime suspect in meltdown'.

In this question, you are being asked to follow an argument, identify implications and recognise inconsistencies:

2. According to the article, what is happening to the ice in the Arctic, and why?

(8 marks)

You now have to compare the two items.

3. Compare the two articles, examining:
   - their attitudes to the melting ice
   - how they use fact and opinion
   - the language used.

(11 marks)

SECTION B: WRITING TO ARGUE, PERSUADE OR ADVISE

Answer **one** question from this section.
Spend about **45 minutes** on this section.
You may use some of the information from Section A if you wish, but you do not have to do so.
If you use any of the information, do not simply copy it.

Remember:
- spend 5–10 minutes planning and sequencing your material
- try to write one and a half to two sides for your answer
- spend five minutes checking:
  - your paragraphing
  - your punctuation
  - your spelling.

Either

4. Write a letter to *The Independent on Sunday* to **argue** that we concentrate too much on food and drink fads, and should pay more attention to serious issues.

(27 marks)

Or

5. Write an article for your school magazine, to **persuade** students to join the school's Environmental Protection Group.

   You might wish to include information on:
   - how the group is organised
   - what activities it has been involved in
   - plans for the future.

(27 marks)

Or

6. Write the text of a speech, to be given to your year group, to **advise** them to avoid the lure of advertisers and the products they promote.

(27 marks)

Or

7. Write the text for a leaflet about lifestyle, aimed at young adults, in which you:

   argue that a healthy lifestyle increases happiness
   and
   offer **advice** on how they can make improvements to the way they live.

(27 marks)

Item 1

ICEBERG IN A BOTTLE SET TO WASH OVER UK

by Nikola Medic and Geoffrey Lean

Brace yourself for the latest mineral water fad: bottled iceberg. Soon drinkers in the UK will be able to enjoy the, er, coolest non-alcoholic drink of all.

A Newfoundland company, which sells iceberg water through Canada's largest supermarket chain, is planning to begin exporting it to Britain by late June, with a one-litre bottle costing about £1.20. The somewhat confusingly named Canadian Iceberg Corporation of America is the first in the world to harvest the floating frozen masses for human consumption.

Every year 40 000 icebergs break off the Greenland coast and drift south towards Newfoundland, an island off Canada's eastern seaboard. The corporation has been licensed by the Canadian government to catch and sell them.

Ronald Stamp, a former fish wholesaler, started the business in the early 1990s. He would chase icebergs up and down the coast in a boat, brandishing a chainsaw lubricated with vegetable oil, and hack bits off them. He then tried another method: waiting until the bergs smashed themselves to pieces on the island's rocky shores and then scooping chunks of the ice aboard a trawler with a net.

His big break came when he joined forces with the owner of a water-bottling business, Paul Benson. The pair invested in a barge equipped with ice crushers, heated tanks, an excavator arm and a grapple.

Now the business corrals its chosen icebergs near the coast, trying to ground them on the seabed. "An iceberg is like a mountain bouncing in the water," says Mr Stamp. "It's dense like concrete, and has a tendency to flip over without warning."

Once they have caught their berg, speed is the key to the harvest. The grapple – a pair of metal jaws normally used to take bites of granite in quarries – grabs a chunk of ice weighing half a ton and delivers it to the ice grinders. Then it goes to the heating tanks where the water melts while the barge heads for land and docks. Finally the water is bottled and sold under the name Borealis, after the Northern Lights.

Mr Stamp, who hopes to expand the business worldwide, envisages abandoning the barge for an ocean-going factory capable of bottling the freshly harvested water on the chilly spot. At present the company only goes to sea once or twice a year between April and December (the whole coast is frozen during the winter). He reckons that this will eventually increase to seven expeditions.

And with icebergs weighing millions of tons and containing enough water to supply a city of 150 000 people for a year, there is little chance of the company running out of supplies.

Item 2

Back Forward Stop Refresh Home AutoFill Print Mail

Address: go

Lycoos : Your Personal Internet Guide 2idesign mnemonic9

Favorites History Search Scrapbook Page Holder

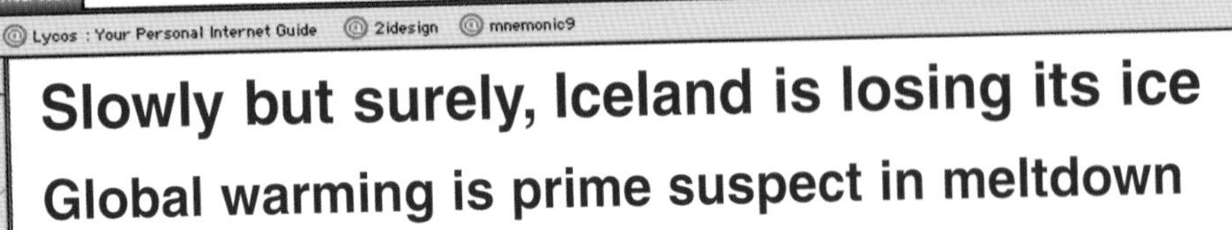

Slowly but surely, Iceland is losing its ice

Global warming is prime suspect in meltdown

Colin Woodard

Jokulsarlon, Iceland – from the gravelly, newborn shores of this frigid lagoon, Iceland's Vatnajokull ice cap is breathtaking.

The vast dome of snow and ice descends from angry clouds to smother jagged 3000-foot-tall mountains. Then it spills out from the peaks in a steep outlet glacier 9.3 miles wide and 12.4 miles long – an insignificant appendage of Europe's largest ice cap despite its impressive size.

A hundred years ago, however, there was no lagoon here. The shoreline was under 100 feet of glacial ice. The outlet glacier, known as Breidamerkurjokull, extended to within 250 yards of the ocean, having crushed medieval farms and fields in its path during the preceding centuries, a time now referred to as the Little Ice Age.

Today, Breidamerkurjokull's massive snout ends about two miles from the ocean. In its hasty retreat, the glacier has left the rapidly expanding lagoon, which is filled with icebergs calved from its front. The lagoon is 350 feet deep and has nearly doubled its size during the past decade. Every year, it grows larger, threatening to wash out Iceland's main highway.

There is no doubt about it: Iceland and much of the rest of the Arctic and Sub-Arctic regions are warming up.

Average winter surface temperatures in the Arctic have increased by two degrees centigrade during the past century, melting ice caps, glaciers, sea ice and permafrost.

During the past two years, researchers have concluded that:

- Arctic sea ice shrank by 14 400 square miles per year from 1978 to 1998, a 6 per cent reduction overall.
- Sea ice thinned by about 40 per cent in recent decades, from an average of 10.2 feet in the period from 1958 to 1976 to about 5.9 feet from 1993 to 1997. Current thinning is estimated at about 4 inches a year.
- Since 1993, the Greenland ice cap – the Arctic's largest – has thinned by more than 3 feet a year on its southern and eastern edges.
- Permafrost is thawing across Alaska. Near Barrow, permafrost was 8 to 10 inches thinner from 1991 to 1997 than it was from 1964 to 1968.
- Iceland, which brushes against the Arctic Circle, has seen a 0.5 to 1 degree Fahrenheit rise in average summer temperatures since the early 1980s. The glaciers that cover 11 per cent of the country have been in rapid retreat since 1995.

And in an unprecedented development reported late last week, an ice-free patch of ocean about a mile wide has opened at the North Pole.

Scientists think the changes are coming in part from global warming caused by greenhouse gas emissions from cars, factories and burning rainforests. But researchers cannot be certain.

Many of the researchers who made the recent discoveries point out that there are large variations in the

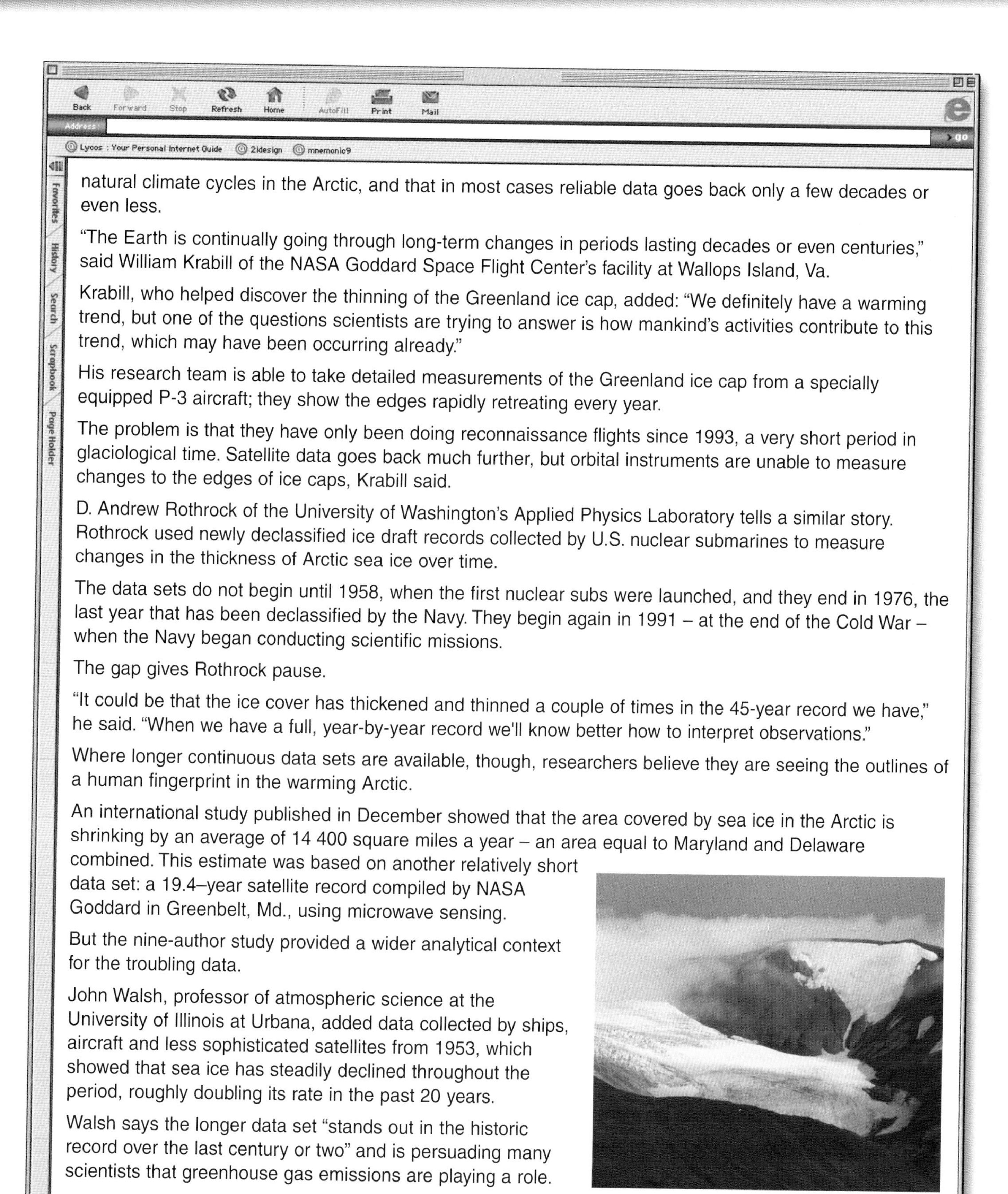

natural climate cycles in the Arctic, and that in most cases reliable data goes back only a few decades or even less.

"The Earth is continually going through long-term changes in periods lasting decades or even centuries," said William Krabill of the NASA Goddard Space Flight Center's facility at Wallops Island, Va.

Krabill, who helped discover the thinning of the Greenland ice cap, added: "We definitely have a warming trend, but one of the questions scientists are trying to answer is how mankind's activities contribute to this trend, which may have been occurring already."

His research team is able to take detailed measurements of the Greenland ice cap from a specially equipped P-3 aircraft; they show the edges rapidly retreating every year.

The problem is that they have only been doing reconnaissance flights since 1993, a very short period in glaciological time. Satellite data goes back much further, but orbital instruments are unable to measure changes to the edges of ice caps, Krabill said.

D. Andrew Rothrock of the University of Washington's Applied Physics Laboratory tells a similar story. Rothrock used newly declassified ice draft records collected by U.S. nuclear submarines to measure changes in the thickness of Arctic sea ice over time.

The data sets do not begin until 1958, when the first nuclear subs were launched, and they end in 1976, the last year that has been declassified by the Navy. They begin again in 1991 – at the end of the Cold War – when the Navy began conducting scientific missions.

The gap gives Rothrock pause.

"It could be that the ice cover has thickened and thinned a couple of times in the 45-year record we have," he said. "When we have a full, year-by-year record we'll know better how to interpret observations."

Where longer continuous data sets are available, though, researchers believe they are seeing the outlines of a human fingerprint in the warming Arctic.

An international study published in December showed that the area covered by sea ice in the Arctic is shrinking by an average of 14 400 square miles a year – an area equal to Maryland and Delaware combined. This estimate was based on another relatively short data set: a 19.4–year satellite record compiled by NASA Goddard in Greenbelt, Md., using microwave sensing.

But the nine-author study provided a wider analytical context for the troubling data.

John Walsh, professor of atmospheric science at the University of Illinois at Urbana, added data collected by ships, aircraft and less sophisticated satellites from 1953, which showed that sea ice has steadily declined throughout the period, roughly doubling its rate in the past 20 years.

Walsh says the longer data set "stands out in the historic record over the last century or two" and is persuading many scientists that greenhouse gas emissions are playing a role.

General Certificate of Secondary Education
Practice Paper

ENGLISH A
Paper 2

In addition to this paper you will require:

- a copy of the 2004 AQA *Anthology* which you have been studying.

Time allowed: 1 hour 30 minutes

Instructions

- Use blue or black ink.
- Answer **one** question from **Section A** (Poems from different cultures and traditions).
- Answer **one** question from **Section B** (Writing to inform, explain and describe).
- Spend about 45 minutes on each section.
- You must not use a dictionary in this examination.

Information

- The maximum mark for this paper is 54.
- Mark allocations are shown in brackets.
- You are reminded of the need for good English and clear presentation in your answers.
- All questions should be answered in continuous prose. Quality of written communication will be assessed in the answer to Section B.

SECTION A: READING

This section relates to Section 1 of the 2004 AQA *Anthology* that you have been using during the course.

Answer **one** question from this section on the cluster of poems you have studied.
Spend about **45 minutes** on this section.

Either

1. 'Island Man' explores the experience of living in a culture without really feeling a part of it. Compare it with one or more poems that examine this theme of social and cultural exclusion.

(27 marks)

Or

2. Compare 'Love After Love' with one or more poems that you feel has important things to say. Write about:
   - what each poet has to say
   - the way the poets use language
   - how the poets organise their ideas.

(27 marks)

SECTION B: WRITING TO INFORM, EXPLAIN OR DESCRIBE

Answer **one** question in this section.
Spend about **45 minutes** on this section.

Either

3. Write an article for your school newsletter informing readers of the main events of last term.

(27 marks)

Or

4. Explain some of the things young people can do to make the most of their teenage years.

(27 marks)

Or

5. Describe the scene in your house on a typical weekday morning.

(27 marks)

Glossary

abbreviation
a shortened version of a word or group of words.

accent
features of pronunciation that vary according to the speaker's regional or social origin.

alliteration
a phrase where adjacent or closely connected words begin with the same sound, like *'Super Sale!'*

anecdote
a brief account of an (often amusing) incident used to illustrate a point.

annotate
an annotated text is one that has been written on, underlined, highlighted and so on, in order to emphasise important points.

appropriate references
appropriate references are those that focus clearly only on those details required to make a specific point.

appropriate style
the style of a text should be appropriate for its audience. An informal style, for example, would be appropriate for a letter to a friend but probably not for a letter to a potential employer who you haven't met.

Assessment Objectives
the separate skills students must demonstrate to an examiner. The more successfully you meet the Assessment Objectives, the higher your grade.

audience
the people addressed by a text. The term refers to listeners, readers of books, film or TV audiences and users of information technology.

colloquialisms
aspects of language used in familiar and informal situations, often creating a relaxed and chatty mood.

conditional phrase
a phrase in which one thing is dependent upon another. For example, *'I'll see you if I have time'*.

contraction
a word that has been shortened or two words that have been made into one. Often a feature of informal texts.

convention
written English obeys certain 'rules' of spelling, punctuation and grammar that enable us to communicate clearly with one another. Writers sometimes manipulate or break these conventions in order to startle a reader and focus attention on a particular part of a text.

convey
a word often used in exam questions that means something close to communicate or 'get across'. When you are asked how a text conveys ideas you should concentrate on the various techniques (linguistic, structural and presentational) it is using to make its message most effective.

cross-references
links between texts that demonstrate differences and similarities between them. Cross-references can refer both to the language and structure of texts.

dialect
a dialect is a variety of language used in a particular area and which is distinguished by certain features of grammar or vocabulary.

discourse markers
words or phrases that signal the direction of a text. The discourse marker *'on the other hand'*, for example, shows that something not yet mentioned is about to be taken into account.

emotive language
language that is designed to make an appeal to a reader's emotions.

engagement
students who engage with a text demonstrate their involvement with it. Engagement is demonstrated when, for example, students question a piece of writing and consider alternative possible meanings.

evidence
evidence is material taken from a text and then used to support an idea or interpretation of what has been written. Quotations and paraphrase are the most commonly used forms of evidence.

figurative language
language that contains imagery (simile, metaphor, personification) in order to create a particular impression or mood.

imagery
use of language to create a vivid sensory image, often visual. Writers frequently use simile, metaphor, personification or unexpected verbs to create this effect.

imperative tone
a tone adopted by a writer who wishes to command or instruct an audience, and uses imperative verbs such as *'Look'*, *'Open'*, and so on.

implication
something that is suggested, rather than simply stated, by a writer. Texts that make implications require their readers to make inferences.

inference
an interpretation made by the reader that has not been directly stated in a text.

insight
readers who show insight demonstrate that they are prepared to read beyond the surface meaning of a text. Insightful readers make inferences that are both original and sustainable.

irony
a form of implication in which a writer signals an opinion (often not a kind one) without stating it directly.

linguistic device
a specialised use of language that enables a writer to draw attention to a text. The use of repetition, rhetorical questions and emotive language are all linguistic devices.

logical sequence
an account or set of ideas presented in such a way that one thing follows on reasonably from another. Logical sequencing is important in ensuring the writer communicates effectively and clearly with an audience.

metaphor
used when a writer describes something as if it were really something else. *'The sea is a hungry dog'* is a description of one thing as if it is another. It creates a different effect from the phrase, *'The sea is rough'*, which is literal. Metaphor is a general term that covers specific forms of imagery such as simile and personification.

modal verbs
modal verbs (such as *may*, *could* and *might*) are useful when a writer wants to express possibility, speculation or uncertainty.

non-Standard English
any variety of English that deviates from the grammar and vocabulary of the standard variety.

organisational technique
a technique (clear sentence structure, use of discourse markers, logical paragraphing) used to make a text legible and well-sequenced for its audience.

paraphrase
the rendition of a phrase, statement or passage in slightly altered language. It is a form of evidence that, like a quotation, should be presented in as brief a form as possible. Unlike a direct quotation, it should sum up information in a new form rather than use the original text.

personification
a form of metaphor in which language relating to human action, motivation or emotion is used to refer to non-human objects.

phonetic transcription
language that is written as it is spoken. Writers who produce phonetic transcriptions are often making a point about the way people judge regional and social accents, or are trying to convey a regional reality.

poetic language
language that contains lots of figurative meaning. In prose texts, poetic language is usually only appropriate in moderation, as it may not be taken seriously in excess.

presentational device
elements of a text that relate to its appearance rather than the language it has used. Italicisation and the use of photographs are both presentational devices.

purpose
the reason a particular text has been produced. It is closely related to the needs of the target audience.

quotation
quotations are sections of a text lifted unchanged into another piece of writing. They provide evidence that can help to make or illustrate a point but they should not be long and rambling.

register
the register of a piece of writing is the tone it communicates to the reader. If the tone is wrong (for example, it is too aggressive or informal for the intended audience) then the purpose of the writing has not been fulfilled.

rhetoric
language used consciously to create a dramatic effect or response, as in the question, *'Do you really believe that this man is innocent?'*

simile
used when a writer wants to create an image in readers' minds by comparing one thing to another. For example, *'The moon is like a dusty coin in the sky.'*

Standard English
Standard English is the variety of English used in public communication, particularly in writing. It is the form generally used in schools and by educated speakers. It is not limited to a particular region and can be spoken with any accent.

stanza
a verse, or set of lines, in poetry.

structural devices
the use of words, sentences and paragraphs (or stanzas) to create an intended effect on the reader. Structural devices are often used by writers when they break normal conventions to create surprise or a sense of the unusual.

text type
a term used to describe a group of texts that share a purpose: for example, to inform, persuade or describe.

topic sentence
the key sentence in a section of text, such as a paragraph, that provides a summary of what the passage is about.

vocabulary
the words selected for a particular text. Careful choice of vocabulary is important in ensuring the text achieves its desired purpose.